The Fallacy of I.Q.

The Fallacy of I.Q.

Edited and with foreword

by

CARL SENNA

THE THIRD PRESS

JOSEPH OKPAKU PUBLISHING CO., INC.
444 CENTRAL PARK WEST
NEW YORK, N.Y. 10025

ACKNOWLEDGEMENTS

I wish to express my special thanks to Miss Brenda Romine, G. G., the administrative staff of Xavier University's Mercedes Hall for the typing of the manuscript, and Miss Sue Holman.

C. S.

Contents

FOREWORD

After Professor Arthur Jensen of Berkeley published his controversial article on I.Q. and race, a presidential cabinet meeting convened on the subject. Shortly afterwards *The Atlantic Monthly* published an article by Harvard Psychologist Richard Herrnstein which professed Jensen's ideas even more rigidly than Jensen himself did.

Jensen's article resurrected an ancient educational question: What contributes most to a person's social position: genetic inheritance or the social and physical environment? Does a child's nature determine his later success or failure in life? It has been an ancient philosopher's riddle. Clearly Jensen's choice was rooted in the Western concepts of familial exclusiveness, racialism, "good breeding," blue and bad blood, distinctions traditionally related in meaning to the words, gens, genes and genius.

Since our world is our way of expressing it, Jensen had nothing to do but apply the definitions of his racialized cultural heritage to his data. This is not to presume that he is a racist. It's just that his Anglo-American sense of identity made him see dark-skinned people as socially different because of their dark skins. Along with the value meanings in the words "Negro" and "white" came the logic of a racist American history that was to guide Jensen in his racial divisions. In the United States public documents have always listed the races as either black, white, or a negligible "other." Given those directions, Jensen had little freedom to see matters otherwise. Necessarily he found two kinds of I.Q. which he defined as two kinds of intelligence. Even scientific facts cannot exist unless they have names. And so, in accepting the arbitrary racial inventions of his culture, Jensen never questioned the popular definitions of race that he had learned.

During the reign of Joseph Stalin, Soviet biologist Trofim D. Lysenko had imposed the dogma in Russian biology—supported by Communist materialist philosophy—that environmental factors affected genetic inheritance. In the United States the initial tendency was for biologists to reject Lysenko's position for a wholly genetic interpretation. This initial reaction was doubtlessly engendered by the contemporary political climate in the United States. (It was the time when the late Senator Joseph McCarthy and extreme anti-Communist sentiment held sway over public opinion. However, with the fading of McCarthyism, biologists have begun to take a more cautious and mixed view.) Presently most biologists feel that the social environment determines hereditary possibilities, even if genetic material is not very much affected by direct social and physical influences. That is to say, when social conditions are propitious for human reproduction, we inherit physical features from our parents. The physical group inheritance—for skin color, or height—is shaped by social and political decisions concerning who lives to have children. But that inherited physical characteristics are rarely affected, or altered, by normal environmental conditions is a rule that only applies to features of the body. Not even physical abilities can be wholly hereditary in origin because they must be demonstrated in cultural terms. Consider a track runner. Is his "racing event" biological? No, not even very much his speed. He must run within the artificial limits of culture to get his time.

While nothing cultural can be inherited, Jensen, in brief, tries to use statistical analysis to separate the ratio of cultural factors from the genetic ones which determine I.Q. differences between various populations. But the basis for his primary division among people is always a color prejudice.

In short Jensen believes that the I.Q. is a heritable trait—as heritable, for instance, as height—and that it determines any kind of occupational success that people may end up having.

The sensational aspect of Jensen's theory was his conclusion on the effectiveness of compensatory educational programs for poor black people. He guessed that the average lower I.Q. score for American Negroes (as compared to the averages for whites and American Orientals) was the result of heredity rather than social and racial oppression. Since hereditary characteristics are very little affected by the social environment, and postulating that I.Q. was hereditary and predicted absolute potential for learning, Jensen concluded that learning ability (as indicated by I.Q.) could not be improved through special educational programs. He then made his logic even more devastating. He called upon the government to "upgrade" the average I.Q. of the country through eugenic planning and marriage controls. In his eugenic proposal there was, inevitably, a strong totalitarian suggestion and so he met a barrage of political criticism.

The extreme public sensitivity to this issue had already been stimulated by two other controversial documents. During the mid-sixties, then Assistant Secretary of Labor, Daniel P. Moynihan, wrote a provacative secret study of the Negro family. It argued that because of slavery and racial discrimination the black family structure had been rapidly deteriorating in the large urban slums of the North. Moynihan wrote that the Negro family had evolved into a matriarchal dominated unit: Negro males, so he claimed, exhibited an almost "genetically" bred disposition for unemployment, family desertion, crime and social failure; nearly a fourth of all Negro families, in contrast to a fraction of white families, were headed by females. The report vaguely alluded to a possible "genetic fatigue" among blacks so that as a consequence they produced fewer bright individuals today than they had as slaves. Borrowing a phrase made popular by the late anthropologist, Oscar Lewis, Moynihan described the Negro slums as sealed in "a culture of poverty." He concluded that the government could not help most Negro families escape the slums unless extraordinary, possibly, unconstitutional, measures were instituted—as, for example, a guaranteed annual income. While his statistics could not be challenged, Moynihan's interpretations were an ambitious politician's rationalizations for white racism. Of course no one with any good intentions could describe either the author or his report as racist. Nonetheless, in seeing blacks as only having educational and income level differences, the Report was vague and useless. Moynihan, like Jensen, was trapped in the Anglo view of history. That is to say, non-racial differences (with the exception of income and education) between American blacks (which are the same as between American whites) were totally ignored. One concluded from Moynihan's Report that religious, political and cultural differences among Afro-Americans had no influence upon variations in family stability, educational achievement and class values.

In a speech on the Negro family at Howard University (June 4, 1965) President Lyndon B. Johnson utilized some of Moynihan's facts to stress the need for poverty legislation. Moynihan's secret Report then came to public attention and was later related to that other famous government paper, the Coleman Report.

In a study made over a two year period under a grant from the U.S. Office of Education, John Hopkins Sociology Professor, James S. Coleman, reported that blacks lagged behind whites in scholastic achievement from grades one to twelve. Furthermore this difference became more pronounced with increasing age. Coleman's main finding was that compensatory education methods had little effect upon black academic achievement in comparison to that of whites. Whether it was an integrated or a segregated school system, the academic record for blacks was consistently lower than for whites.

The reasons for the poor academic achievement of black children—always, it must be remembered, in comparison to whites—might have been any number of environmental factors: class attitudes towards education, the relative newness of integrated education, still prevalent negative racial attitudes among both races, or some undetected variable in Negro home life. But Jensen and other hereditarians felt that those reasons seemed remote against a genetic possibility. Again, the hereditarians could not overlook the social implications of skin color. Their racialized values encouraged them towards the genetic-racial view.

So also was Coleman's inability to explain the differences in school performances (between the two colors of children) either in terms of racial heredity or social factors. Since a large number of white children performed below the average achievement levels of black children, one wonders why the hereditarians did not simply add the slow achievers into one group irregardless of color. But this would have only been logical if they believed that race had no social influence upon learning. And Coleman held no such belief. No respectable social scientist claimed that increased melanin heredity lowered one's I.Q. and for most of them, even the denial of such a possibility was beneath serious discussion. As linguist Dr. Noam Chomsky of M.I.T. put it, "The correlation of skin color and height with I.Q. is not a serious scientific field of investigation." In fact, given that racial physique does not determine I.Q., any argument to link the two makes I.Q. socially determined. This can be seen in changing American racial attitudes and new public tolerance of long hair styles among men. The value of people's appearance is an entirely social construction.

At any rate, Jensen published his widely reported piece in the *Harvard Educational Review* (Winter, 1969). Notwithstanding the contradictory evidence of studies on I.Q. and race already published, there was nothing wrong in letting Jensen restate the hereditarian position. But he audaciously took the offensive, almost as if sensing the frailty of his statistical interpolations and a skeptical reception. Instead of pressing simply for the genetic determination of I.Q., he tried to also establish a link between race and I.Q. The issue would have remained strictly a scientific one had he only insisted that an I.Q. was 80% hereditary. But Jensen also claimed that I.Q. heredity manifests itself through skin color. Aside from that preposterous claim, he also suggested that compensatory education could improve scholastic performance but not the I.Q. upon which he assumed high grades depend. His theory had an obvious contradiction that was racially insulting as well. So, although polemics alone cannot be helpful, this debate is no longer strictly academic. Already it can be said with certainty that there is sufficient evidence to refute the notion that an I.Q. cannot significantly vary. The problem, in fact, is the social meaning of I.Q. Is it hereditary? If so, what does that mean? In provoking these questions the controversy has been largely beneficial. Serious scholars have questioned, for the first time, whether there is any educational validity to the notion that the I.Q. is a measure of intelligence, or that an I.Q. really means innate intelligence. In this regard it was rather easy to go beyond refuting the racial link to I.Q. since there were no serious racial definitions to correlate with the statistics. As a matter of fact, the spurious educational values attached to the I.Q. were not much more difficult to demolish.

In this collection of essays the hereditarian estimate of I.Q. heredity is refuted by a biologist and an educational psychologist. The social meaning of I.Q. and what an I.Q. measures is the burden of essays by David Robinson and myself. We also reprint a report by a U.S. Government-sponsored Research Project which answers Jensen's rhetorical question in the title of his *Harvard Educational Review* article. The Milwaukee Study, reported, by Stephen Strickland, demonstrates that I.Q. scores can be significantly raised by intensive educational stimulation. The study also shows that blacks can learn as well in all-black schools as in integrated ones, *if the school facilities, the social and home environments* are nearly the same as for whites. Most people did not have to research this fact but they might not have known that I.Q. scores are largely dependent upon social and cultural stimulation. In a word—such that it can —I.Q. reflects rather than predicts a person's preparation for academic work.

The current higher *average* I.Q. of whites in the United States, which has depended upon white oppression—and which diminishes with the eclipse of white racism—has been interpreted as the *reason* for white political hegemony. Unfortunately many whites used these "reflections" of social and political dominance to support the myth of black genetic mental inferiority. And many blacks discounted the value of the educational methods upon which academic success—and, sometimes, a high I.Q. depends. They had been persuaded by the argument that one needed a high I.Q. to academically succeed, from which it followed (if the I.Q. was static and hereditary) that they could neither improve their social possibilities nor raise their I.Q.

Carl Senna
Boston, Massachusetts

1

RACE AND INTELLIGENCE

BY RICHARD C. LEWONTIN

In the Spring of 1653 Pope Innocent X condemned a perni-
cious heresy which espoused the doctrines of "total depravity,
irresistable grace, lack of free will, predestination and limited
atonement." That heresy was Jansenism and its author was
Cornelius Jansen, Bishop of Ypres.

In the winter of 1969 the same doctrine appeared in the "Harvard Educational Review." That doctrine is now called "jensenism" by the "New York Times Magazine" and its author is Arthur
R. Jensen, professor of educational psychology at the University
of California at Berkeley. It is a doctrine as erroneous in the
twentieth century as it was in the seventeenth. I shall try to
play the Innocent.

Jensen's article, "How Much Can We Boost I.Q. and Scholastic
Achievement?" created such a furor that the "Review" reprinted
it along with critiques by psychologists, theorists of education
and a population geneticist under the title "Environment,
Heredity and Intelligence." The article first came to my attention
when, at no little expense, it was sent to every member of the
National Academy of Sciences by the eminent white Anglo-Saxon
inventor, William Shockley, as part of his continuing campaign
to have the Academy study the effects of inter-racial mating.
It is little wonder that the "New York Times" found the matter
newsworthy, and that Professor Jensen has surely become the
most discussed and least read essayist since Karl Marx. I shall

try, in this article, to display Professor Jensen's argument, to show how the structure of his argument is designed to make his point and to reveal what appear to be deeply embedded assumptions derived from a particular world view, leading him to erroneous conclusions. I shall say little or nothing about the critiques of Jensen's article, which would require even more space to criticize than the original article itself.

THE POSITION

Jensen's argument consists essentially of an elaboration on two incontrovertible facts, a causative explanation and a programmatic conclusion. The two facts are that black people perform, on the average, more poorly than whites on standard I.Q. tests, and that special programs of compensatory education so far tried have not had much success in removing this difference. His causative explanation for these facts is that I.Q. is highly heritable, with most of the variation among individuals arising from genetic rather than environmental sources. His programmatic conclusion is that there is no use in trying to remove the difference in I.Q. by education since it arises chiefly from genetic causes and the best thing that can be done for black children is to capitalize on those skills for which they are biologically adapted. Such a conclusion is so clearly at variance with the present egalitarian consensus and so clearly smacks of a racist elitism, whatever its merit or motivation, that a very careful analysis of the argument is in order.

The article begins with the pronouncement: "Compensatory education has been tried and it apparently has failed." A documentation of that failure and a definition of compensatory education are left to the end of the article for good logical and pedagogical reasons. Having caught our attention by whacking us over the head with a two-by-four, like that famous trainer of mules, Jensen then asks: "What has gone wrong? In other fields, when bridges do not stand, when aircrafts do not fly, when machines do not work, when treatments do not cure, despite all the conscientious efforts on the part of many persons

2

to make them do so, one begins to question the basic assumptions, principles, theories, and hypotheses that guide one's efforts. Is it time to follow suit in education?"

Who can help but answer that last rhetorical question with a resounding "Yes"? What thoughtful and intelligent person can avoid being struck by the intellectual and empirical bankruptcy of educational psychology as it is practiced in our mass educational systems? The innocent reader will immediately fall into close sympathy with Professor Jensen, who, it seems, is about to dissect educational psychology and show it up as a pre-scientific jumble without theoretic coherence or prescriptive competence. But the innocent reader will be wrong. For the rest of Jensen's article puts the blame for the failure of his science not on the scientists but on the children. According to him, it is not that his science and its practitioners have failed utterly to understand human motivation, behavior and development but simply that the damn kids are ineducable.

The unconscious irony of his metaphor of bridges, airplanes and machines has apparently been lost on him. The fact is that in the twentieth century bridges do stand, machines do work and airplanes do fly, because they are built on clearly understood mechanical and hydrodynamic principles which even moderately careful and intelligent engineers can put into practice. In the seventeenth century that was not the case, and the general opinion was that men would never succeed in their attempts to fly because flying was impossible. Jensen proposes that we take the same view of education and that, in the terms of his metaphor, fallen bridges be taken as evidence of the unbridgeability of rivers. The alternative explanation, that educational psychology is still in the seventeenth century, is apparently not part of his philosophy.

This view of technological failure as arising from ontological rather than epistemological sources is a common form of apology at many levels of practice. Anyone who has dealt with plumbers will appreciate how many things "can't be fixed" or "weren't meant to be used like that." Physicists tell me that their failure to formulate an elegant general theory of fundamental particles

3

is a result of there not being any underlying regularity to be discerned. How often men, in their overweening pride, blame nature for their own failures. This professionalist bias, that if a problem were soluble it would have been solved, lies at the basis of Jensen's thesis which can only be appreciated when seen in this light.

Having begun with the assumption that I.Q. cannot be equalized, Jensen now goes on to state why not. He begins his investigation with a discussion of the "nature of intelligence," by which he means the way in which intelligence is defined by testing and the correlation of intelligence test scores with scholastic and occupational performance. A very strong point is made that I.Q. testing was developed in a western industrialized society specifically as a prognostication of success in that society by the generally accepted criteria. He makes a special point of noting that psychologists' notions of status and success have a high correlation with those of the society at large, so that it is entirely reasonable that tests created by psychologists will correlate highly with conventional measures of success. One might think that this argument, that I.Q. testing is "culture bound," would militate against Jensen's general thesis of the biological and specifically genetical basis of I.Q. differences. Indeed, it is an argument often used against I.Q. testing for so-called "deprived" children, since it is supposed that they have developed in a sub-culture that does not prepare them for such tests. What role does this "environmentalist" argument play in Jensen's thesis? Is it simply evidence of his total fairness and objectivity? No. Jensen has seen, more clearly than most, that the argument of the specific cultural origins of I.Q. testing and especially the high correlation of these tests with occupational status cuts both ways. For, if the poorer performance of blacks on I.Q. tests has largely genetic rather than environmental causes, then it follows that blacks are also genetically handicapped for other high status components of Western culture. That is, what Jensen is arguing is that differences between cultures are in large part genetically determined and that I.Q. testing is simply one manifestation of those differences.

4

In this light we can also understand his argument concerning the existence of "general intelligence" as measured by I.Q. tests. Jensen is at some pains to convince his readers that there is a single factor, g, which, in factor analysis of various intelligence tests, accounts for a large fraction of the variance of scores. The existence of such a factor, while not critical to the argument, obviously simplifies it, for then I.Q. tests would really be testing for "something" rather than just being correlated with scholastic and occupational performance. While Jensen denies that intelligence should be reified, he comes perilously close to doing so in his discussion of g.

Without going into factor analysis at any length, I will point out only that factor analysis does not give a unique result for any given set of data. Rather, it gives an infinity of possible results among which the investigator chooses according to his tastes and preconceptions of the models he is fitting. One strategy in factor analysis is to pack as much weight as possible into one factor, while another is to distribute the weights over as many factors as possible as equally as possible. Whether one chooses one of these or some other depends upon one's model, the numerical analysis only providing the weights appropriate for each model. Thus, the impression left by Jensen that factor analysis somehow naturally or ineluctably isolates one factor with high weight is wrong.

"TRUE MERIT"?

In the welter of psychological metaphysics involving concepts of "crystallized" as against "fluid" intelligence, "generalized" intelligence, "intelligence" as opposed to "mental ability," there is some danger of losing sight of Jensen's main point: I.Q. tests are culture bound and there is good reason that they should be, because they are predictors of "culture bound" activities and values. What is further implied, of course, is that those who do not perform well on these tests are less well suited for high status and must paint barns rather than pictures. We read that "We have to face it: the assortment of persons into

5

occupational roles simply is not 'fair' in any absolute sense. The best we can hope for is that true merit, given equality of opportunity, act as a basis for the natural assorting process." What a world view is there revealed! The most rewarding places in society shall go to those with "true merit" and that is the best we can hope for. Of course, Professor Jensen is safe since, despite the abject failure of educational psychology to solve the problems it has set itself, that failure does not arise from lack of "true merit" on the part of psychologists but from the natural intransigence of their human subjects.

Having established that there are differences among men in the degree to which they are adapted to higher status and high satisfaction roles in Western society, and having stated that education has not succeeded in removing these differences, Jensen now moves on to their cause. He raises the question of "fixed" intelligence and quite rightly dismisses it as misleading. He introduces us here to what he regards as the two real issues. "The first issue concerns the genetic basis of individual differences in intelligence; the second concerns the stability or constancy of the I.Q. through the individual's lifetime." Jensen devotes some three-quarters of his essay to an attempt to demonstrate that I.Q. is developmentally rather stable, being to all intents and purposes fixed after the age of eight, and that most of the variation in I.Q. among individuals in the population has a genetic rather than environmental basis. Before looking in detail at some of these arguments, we must again ask where he is headed. While Jensen argues strongly that I.Q. is "culture bound," he wishes to argue that it is not environmentally determined. This is a vital distinction. I.Q. is "culture bound" in the sense that it is related to performance in a Western industrial society. But the determination of the ability to perform culturally defined tasks might itself be entirely genetic. For example, a person suffering from a genetically caused deaf-mutism is handicapped to different extents in cultures requiring different degrees of verbal performance, yet his disorder did not have an environmental origin.

Jensen first dispenses with the question of developmental

6

stability of I.Q. Citing Benjamin Bloom's survey of the literature, he concludes that the correlation between test scores of an individual at different ages is close to unity after the age of eight. The inference to be drawn from this fact is, I suppose, that it is not worth trying to change I.Q. by training after that age. But such an inference cannot be made. All that can be said is that, given the usual progression of educational experience to which most children are exposed, there is sufficient consistency not to cause any remarkable changes in I.Q. That is, a child whose educational experience (in the broad sense) may have ruined his capacity to perform by the age of eight is not likely to experience an environment in his later years that will do much to alter those capacities. Indeed, given the present state of educational theory and practice, there is likely to be a considerable reinforcement of early performance. To say that children do not change their I.Q. is not the same as saying they cannot. Moreover, Jensen is curiously silent on the lower correlation and apparent plasticity of I.Q. at younger ages, which is after all the chief point of Bloom's work.

THE GENETIC ARGUMENT

The heart of Jensen's paper is contained in his long discussion of the distribution and inheritance of intelligence. Clearly he feels that here his main point is to be established. The failure of compensatory education, the developmental stability of I.Q., the obvious difference between the performance of blacks and whites can be best understood, he believes, when the full impact of the findings of genetics is felt. In his view, insufficient attention has been given by social scientists to the findings of geneticists, and I must agree with him. Although there are exceptions, there has been a strong professional bias toward the assumption that human behavior is infinitely plastic, a bias natural enough in men whose professional commitment is to changing behavior. It is as a reaction to this tradition, and as a natural outcome of his confrontation with the failure of educational psychology, that Jensen's own opposite bias flows, as I have already claimed.

7

The first step in his genetical argument is the demonstration that I.Q. scores are normally distributed or nearly so. I am unable to find in his paper any explicit statement of why he regards this point as so important. From repeated references to Sir Francis Galton, filial regression, mutant genes, a few major genes for exceptional ability and assortative mating, it gradually emerges that an underlying normality of the distribution appears to Jensen as an important consequence of genetic control of I.Q. He asks: ". . . is intelligence itself—not just our measurements of it—really normally distributed?" Apparently he believes that if intelligence, quite aside from measurement, were really normally distributed, this would demonstrate its biological and genetical status. Aside from a serious epistemological error involved in the question, the basis for his concern is itself erroneous. There is nothing in genetic theory that requires or even suggests that a phenotypic character should be normally distributed, even when it is completely determined genetically. Depending upon the degree of dominance of genes, interaction between them, frequencies of alternative alleles at the various gene loci in the population and allometric growth relations between various parts of the organism transforming primary gene effects, a character may have almost any uni-modal distribution and under some circumstances even a multi-modal one.

After establishing the near-normality of the curve of I.Q. scores, Jensen goes directly to a discussion of the genetics of continuously varying characters. He begins by quoting with approbation E. L. Thorndike's maxim: "In the actual race of life, which is not to get ahead, but to get ahead of somebody, the chief determining factor is heredity." This quotation along with many others used by Jensen shows a style of argument that is not congenial to natural scientists, however it may be a part of other disciplines. There is a great deal of appeal to authority and the acceptance of the empirically unsubstantiated opinions of eminent authorities as a kind of relevant evidence. We hear of "three eminent geneticists," or "the most distinguished exponent (of genetical methods), Sir Cyril Burt." The irrelevance of this kind of argument is illustrated precisely by

8

the appeal to E. L. Thorndike, who, despite his eminence in the history of psychology, made the statement quoted by Jensen in 1905, when nothing was known about genetics outside of attempts to confirm Mendel's paper. Whatever the eventual truth of his statement turns out to be, Thorndike made it out of his utter ignorance of the genetics of human behavior, and it can only be ascribed to the sheer prejudice of a Methodist Yankee.

HERITABILITY

To understand the main genetical argument of Jensen, we must dwell, as he does, on the concept of heritability. We cannot speak of a trait being molded by heredity, as opposed to environment. Every character of an organism is the result of a unique interaction between the inherited genetic information and the sequence of environments through which the organism has passed during its development. For some traits the variations in environment have little effect, so that once the genotype is known, the eventual form of the organism is pretty well specified. For other traits, specification of the genetic make-up may be a very poor predictor of the eventual phenotype because even the smallest environmental effects may affect the trait greatly. But for all traits there is a many-many relationship between gene and character and between environment and character. Only by a specification of both the genotype and the environmental sequence can the character be predicted. Nevertheless, traits do vary in the degree of their genetic determination and this degree can be expressed, among other ways, by their heritabilities.

The distribution of the character values, say I.Q. scores, in a population arises from a mixture of a large number of genotypes. Each genotype in the population does not have a unique phenotype corresponding to it because the different individuals of that genotype have undergone somewhat different environmental sequences in their development. Thus, each genotype has a distribution of I.Q. scores associated with it. Some genotypes are more common in the population so their distributions

9

contribute heavily to determining the over-all distribution, while others are rare and make little contribution. The total variation in the population, as measured by the variance, results from the variation between the mean I.Q. scores of the different genotypes and the variation around each genotypic mean. The heritability of a measurement is defined as the ratio of the variance due to the differences between the genotypes to the total variance in the population. If this heritability were 1.0, it would mean that all the variation in the population resulted from differences between genotypes but that there was no environmentally caused variation around each genotypic mean. On the other hand, a heritability of 0.0 would mean that there was no genetic variation because all individuals were effectively identical in their genes, and that all the variation in the population arose from the environmental differences in the development of the different individuals.

Defined in this way, heritability is not a concept that can be applied to a trait in general, but only to a trait in a particular set of environments. Thus, different populations may have more or less genetic variation for the same character. Moreover, a character may be relatively insensitive to environment in a particular environmental range, but be extremely sensitive outside this range. Many such characters are known, and it is the commonest kind of relation between character and environment. Finally, some genotypes are more sensitive to environmental fluctuation than others so that two populations with the same genetic variance but different genotypes, and living in the same environments, may still have different heritabilities for a trait.

The estimation of heritability of a trait in a population depends on measuring individuals of known degrees of relationship to each other and comparing the observed correlation in the trait between relatives with the theoretical correlation from genetic theory. There are two difficulties that arise in such a procedure. First, the exact theoretical correlation between relatives, except for identical twins, cannot be specified unless there is detailed knowledge of the mode of inheritance of the character. A first order approximation is possible, however, based upon some simplifying assumptions, and it is unusual for this approximation to be badly off.

A much more serious difficulty arises because relatives are correlated not only in their heredities but also in their environments. Two sibs are much more alike in the sequence of environments in which they developed than are two cousins or two unrelated persons. As a result there will be an overestimate of the heritability of a character, arising from the added correlation between relatives from environmental similarities. There is no easy way to get around this bias in general, so that great weight must be put on peculiar situations in which the ordinary environmental correlations are disturbed. That is why so much emphasis is placed, in human genetics, on the handful of cases of identical twins raised apart from birth, and the much more numerous cases of totally unrelated children raised in the same family. Neither of these cases is completely reliable, however, since twins separated from birth are nevertheless likely to be raised in families belonging to the same socio-economic, racial, religious and ethnic categories, while unrelated children raised in the same family may easily be treated rather more differently than biological sibs. Despite these difficulties, the weight of evidence from a variety of correlations between relatives puts the heritability of I.Q. in various human populations between .6 and .8. For reasons of his argument, Jensen prefers the higher value but it is not worth quibbling over. Volumes could be written on the evaluation of heritability estimates for I.Q. and one can find a number of faults with Jensen's treatment of the published data. However, it is irrelevant to questions of the failure of compensatory education, whether the heritability of I.Q. is .4 or .8, so I shall accept Jensen's rather high estimate without serious argument.

The description I have given of heritability, its application to a specific population in a specific set of environments and the difficulties in its accurate estimation are all discussed by Jensen. While the emphasis he gives to various points differs from mine, and his estimate of heritability is on the high side, he appears to have said in one way or another just about every-

11

thing that a judicious man can say. The very judiciousness of his argument has been disarming to geneticists especially, and they have failed to note the extraordinary conclusions that are drawn from these reasonable premises. Indeed, the logical and empirical hiatus between the conclusions and the premises is especially striking and thought-provoking in view of Jensen's apparent understanding of the technical issues.

The first conclusion concerns the cause of the difference between the I.Q. distributions of blacks and whites. On the average, over a number of studies, blacks have a distribution of I.Q. scores whose mean is about 15 points—about 1 standard deviation—below whites. Taking into account the lower variance of scores among blacks than among whites, this difference means that about 11 percent of blacks have I.Q. scores above the mean white score (as compared with 50 percent of whites) while 18 percent of whites score below the mean black score (again, as compared to 50 percent of blacks). If, according to Jensen, "gross socio-economic factors" are equalized between the tested groups, the difference in means is reduced to 11 points. It is hard to know what to say about overlap between the groups after this correction, since the standard deviations of such equalized populations will be lower. From these and related observations, (and the estimate is .8 for the heritability of I.Q. in white populations, no reliable estimate existing for blacks), Jensen concludes that:

". . . all we are left with are various lines of evidence, no one of which is definitive alone, but which, viewed altogether, make it a not unreasonable hypothesis that genetic factors are strongly implicated in the average Negro-white intelligence difference. The preponderance of evidence is less consistent with a strictly environmental hypothesis than with a genetic hypothesis, which of course, does not exclude the influence of environment on its interaction with genetic factors."

Anyone not familiar with the standard litany of academic disclaimers ("not unreasonable hypothesis," "does not exclude," "in my opinion") will, taking this statement at face value, find nothing to disagree with since it says nothing. To contrast a "strictly environmental hypothesis" with "a genetic hypothesis which . . . does not exclude the influence of the environment" is to be guilty of the utmost triviality. If that is the only conclusion he means to come to, Jensen has just wasted a great deal of space in the "Harvard Educational Review." But of course, like all cant, the special language of the social scientist needs to be translated into common English. What Jensen is saying is: "It is pretty clear, although not absolutely proved, that most of the differences in I.Q. between blacks and whites is genetical." This, at least, is not a trivial conclusion. Indeed, it may even be true. However, the evidence offered by Jensen is irrelevant.

IS IT LIKELY?

How can that be? We have admitted the high heritability of I.Q. and the reality of the difference between the black and the white distributions. Moreover, we have seen that adjustment for gross socio-economic level still leaves a large difference. Is it not then likely that the difference is genetic? No. It is neither likely nor unlikely. There is no evidence. The fundamental error of Jensen's argument is to confuse heritability of a character within a population with heritability of the difference between two populations. Indeed, between two populations, the concept of heritability of their difference is meaningless. This is because a variance based upon two measurements has only one degree of freedom and so cannot be partitioned into genetic and environmental components. The genetic basis of the differences between two populations bears no logical or empirical relation to the heritability within populations and cannot be inferred from it, as I will show in a simple but realistic example. In addition, the notion that eliminating what appear a priori to be major environmental variables will serve to eliminate a large part of the environmentally caused difference between the populations is biologically naive. In the context of I.Q. testing, it assumes that educational psychologists know what the major sources of environmental difference between black and white performance are. Thus, Jensen compares blacks with American

13

Indians whom he regards as far more environmentally disadvantaged. But a priori judgements of the importance of different aspects of the environment are valueless, as every ecologist and plant physiologist knows. My example will speak to that point as well.

Let us take two completely inbred lines of corn. Because they are completely inbred by self-fertilization, there is no genetic variation in either line, but the two lines will be genetically different from each other. Let us now plant seeds of these two inbred lines in flower pots with ordinary potting soil, one seed of each line to a pot. After they have germinated and grown for a few weeks we will measure the height of each plant. We will discover variation in height from plant to plant. Because each line is completely inbred, the variation in height within lines must be entirely environmental, a result of variation in potting conditions from pot to pot. Then the heritability of plant height in both lines is 0.0. But there will be an average difference in plant height between lines that arises entirely from the fact that the two lines are genetically different. Thus the difference between lines is entirely genetical even though the heritability of height is 0!

Now let us do the opposite experiment. We will take two handfuls from a sack containing seed of an open-pollinated variety of corn. Such a variety has lots of genetic variation in it. Instead of using potting soil, however, we will grow the seed in vermiculite watered with a carefully made up nutrient, Knop's solution, used by plant physiologists for controlled growth experiments. One batch of seed will be grown on complete Knop's solution, but the other will have the concentration of nitrates cut in half and, in addition, we will leave out the minute trace of zinc salt that is part of the necessary trace elements (30 parts per billion). After several weeks we will measure the plants. Now we will find variation within seed lots which is entirely genetical since no environmental variation within lots was allowed. Thus heritability will be 1.0. However, there will be a radical difference between seed lots which is ascribable entirely to the difference in nutrient levels. Thus, we have a case where heritability within populations is complete, yet the difference between populations is entirely environmental!

But let us carry our experiment to the end. Suppose we do not know about the difference in the nutrient solutions because it was really the carelessness of our assistant that was involved. We call in a friend who is a very careful chemist and ask him to look into the matter for us. He analyzes the nutrient solutions and discovers the obvious—only half as much nitrates in the case of the stunted plants. So we add the missing nitrates and do the experiment again. This time our second batch of plants will grow a little larger but not much, and we will conclude that the difference between the lots is genetic since equalizing the large difference in nitrate level had so little effect. But, of course, we would be wrong for it is the missing trace of zinc that is the real culprit. Finally, it should be pointed out that it took many years before the importance of minute trace elements in plant physiology was worked out because ordinary laboratory glassware will leach out enough of many trace elements to let plants grow normally. Should educational psychologists study plant physiology?

Having disposed, I hope, of Jensen's conclusion that the high heritability of I.Q. and the lack of effect of correction for gross socio-economic class are presumptive evidence for the genetic basis of the difference between blacks and whites, I will turn to his second erroneous conclusion. The article under discussion began with the observation, which he documents, that compensatory education for the disadvantaged (blacks, chiefly) has failed. The explanation offered for the failure is that I.Q. has a high heritability and that therefore the difference between the races is also mostly genetical. Given that the racial difference is genetical, then environmental change and educational effort cannot make much difference and cannot close the gap very much between blacks and whites. I have already argued that there is no evidence one way or the other about the genetics of interracial I.Q. differences. To understand Jensen's second error, however, we will suppose that the difference is indeed genetical. Let it be entirely genetical. Does this mean that compensatory

15

education, having failed, must fail? The supposition that it must arises from a misapprehension about the fixity of genetically determined traits. It was thought at one time that genetic disorders, because they were genetic, were incurable. Yet we now know that inborn errors of metabolism are indeed curable if their biochemistry is sufficiently well understood and if deficient metabolic products can be supplied exogenously. Yet in the normal range of environments, these inborn errors manifest themselves irrespective of the usual environmental variables. That is, even though no environment in the normal range has an effect on the character, there may be special environments, created in response to our knowledge of the underlying biology of a character, which are effective in altering it.

But we do not need recourse to abnormalities of development to see this point. Jensen says that "there is no reason to believe that the I.Q.'s of deprived children, given an environment of abundance, would rise to a higher level than the already privileged children's I.Q.'s." It is empirically wrong to argue that if the richest environmental experience we can conceive does not raise I.Q. substantially, that we have exhausted the environmental possibilities. In the seventeenth century the infant mortality rates were many times their present level at all socio-economic levels. Using what was then the normal range of environments, the infant mortality rate of the highest socio-economic class would have been regarded as the limit below which one could not reasonably expect to reduce the death rate. But changes in sanitation, public health and disease control—changes which are commonplace to us now but would have seemed incredible to a man of the seventeenth century—have reduced the infant mortality rates of "disadvantaged" urban Americans well below those of even the richest members of seventeenth century society. The argument that compensatory education is hopeless is equivalent to saying that changing 'the form of the seventeenth century gutter would not have a pronounced effect on public sanitation. What compensatory education will be able to accomplish when the study of human behavior finally emerges from its pre-scientific era is anyone's

16

guess. It will be most extraordinary if it stands as the sole exception to the rule that technological progress exceeds by manifold what even the most optimistic might have imagined.

The real issue in compensatory education does not lie in the heritability of I.Q. or in the possible limits of educational technology. On the reasonable assumption that ways of significantly altering mental capacities can be developed, if it is important enough to do so, the real issue is what the goals of our society will be. Do we want to foster a society in which the "race of life" is "to get ahead of somebody" and in which "true merit," be it genetically or environmentally determined, will be the criterion of men's earthly reward? Or do we want a society in which every man can aspire to the fullest measure of psychic and material fulfillment that social activity can produce? Professor Jensen has made it fairly clear to me what sort of society he wants.

I oppose him.

2

IF YOU'RE SO RICH, YOU MUST BE SMART:
Some thoughts on status, race, and I.Q.

BY DAVID Z. ROBINSON

"When I use a word," Humpty Dumpty said . . . , "it means just what I choose it to mean, neither more nor less."
"The question is," said Alice, "whether you can make words to mean so many different things."
"The question is," said Humpty Dumpty, "which is to be master— that's all."

Lewis Carroll, Through The Looking-Glass

"Thou shalt not answer questionnaires
Or quizzes upon World-Affairs,
   Nor with compliance
Take any test. Thou shalt not sit
With statisticians nor commit
   A social science."

W. H. Auden, Under Which Lyre.

The interaction of race, class, heredity and I.Q. has been a perennial subject of argument among psychologists, and it is tempting to speculate as to why the intellectual community and, to some extent, the popular press have joined in the debate at this time.

I would suggest that the social scientist who postulates that social standing is based on I.Q. plays the same role as the European political theorists of the 19th Century who justified the status of the aristocracy on racial grounds, or the American

Calvinist ministers who insisted that wealth was a sign of the grace of God. The new elite, like the old, feels more comfortable if its status derives from a natural superiority, from "better genes." In particular, as the 1960's have forced the nation to acknowledge the evils of segregation and the realities of black repression, any rationale which puts the blame for limited achievement or low social standing on the black minority finds a ready audience.

I would contend that the theses of Jensen and Herrnstein—while comforting—do not accord to the facts of modern genetics and the observable workings of American society. Such facts and observations suggest three quite different conclusions:

(1) I.Q. is a questionable measure of general intelligence and a minor determinant of success;

(2) Average differences in I.Q. between blacks and whites can never be conclusively ascribed to heredity until blacks and whites get equal treatment in our society;

(3) If a permanent lower class (a caste system) should develop, inheritance of I.Q. will have a very small role compared to "inheritance" of social standing and occupation.

INHERITANCE OF GENES

Genes come in pairs. One of each pair comes from the mother, and one from the father. Only half of a parent's genes are passed on to a child; that child does not inherit—and can never pass on—the genes from the other half.

Although certain characteristics are affected by a single gene pair (e.g., one pair affects sickle-cell anemia, one pair affects the inheritance of PKU disease), other characteristics—I.Q., athletic ability, appearance—are affected by the actions of a rather large number of pairs.

The array of genes that an individual has is called his *genotype*. The totality of his characteristics geneticists call his *phenotype*. A person's actual height or skin color or strength is part of his phenotype and is determined by the joint action of his genotype and the environment.

It is very hard to keep straight in a discussion of genetics the fact that *both* genes and environment are intricately involved in determining human characteristics. For example, height is strongly genetically determined, but even there we know that nutrition and other factors can have a great effect. One cannot say that a child has genes that will determine his height, such as that he will be six feet tall. One must assume a standard environment, and then say that in *that* environment, his genes will make him six feet tall. In a more favorable environment, he might be taller; in a less favorable one, shorter. With a complex polygenic trait like height, it is even possible that environment can affect *relative* size, with the taller of a pair in one environment being the shorter of the pair in another environment.

A person of average I.Q. may be someone with a high I.Q. genotype and a disadvantageous environment; he may have an average genotype with an average environment, or he may have a low I.Q. genotype with an advantageous environment. It is extremely difficult to allocate the contribution of genes alone, and to some people it does not make sense to do so. It is sometimes possible (for example, through experiments with identical twins) to determine how much the variation in a particular characteristic is related to heredity, but then only for particular populations, that is, those that match the twins involved.

For the purpose of understanding the "inheritance" of I.Q., let us assume that the environment of each individual is identical.

1. The *average* I.Q. of children in a family will be the average of the I.Q. of the parents.

2. The *variation* in I.Q. among children in the same family will be fairly wide.* In fact, the average variation in I.Q. of the children in a single family around its mean (about 15 points) is the same as the average variation in the population as a whole.

3. The only significant genetic factor in determining the I.Q.

---

* Conclusions on intrafamily variation depend upon assumptions regarding the total number of genes involved, the way each possible gene in a gene pair affects the I.Q., and the particular way in which particular genes are distributed in the individual parents.

of the children in the family will be the I.Q. of the parents. The grandparents' I.Q., or the average I.Q. of the particular population group from which the children come has no effect (other than the effect they had on determining the parents' I.Q.). One does not inherit genes from a 'stock' or a population, but rather from two individuals with particular genotypes.

THE NATURE OF PHYSICAL ABILITY

When my two boys were younger, they would play football with each other in the yard. One would run with the ball and try to elude the other. This game might be called one-on-one football.

It would be feasible to determine a measure of ability of children to play one-on-one football by taking them into the laboratory and measuring certain of their physical and mental capabilities. Such a series of tests might measure running speed, strength, quickness of response, anticipation, coordination, peripheral vision, and I.Q.

One could take these various measures (and others), weight them appropriately and match people up on a scale. Let us call this scale the Football Quotient (F.Q.). To validate the F.Q., one would take people with different F.Q.'s and test them against each other and see who won the game of one-on-one. One might find the first time around that speed had been weighted too highly and strength too low. The tests and their weights could be changed, but eventually a good system for predicting performance in one-on-one football might emerge.

If we lived in a society that valued success in one-on-one football, every child would have his F.Q. measured and updated as he approached maturity.

Now we *do* live in a country which enjoys pro football, a team game in which the offense has ten types of players (fullback, halfback, quarterback, flanker, center, guard, tackle, tight end, placekicker, punter) and the defense has seven different positions (end, tackle, middle line-backer, outside line-backer, cornerback, strong safety and free safety).

21

Suppose college football didn't exist and coaches had to choose players raw as it were from the population reaching full growth?

In approaching such choices, a person's F.Q. might be somewhat useful, in that there would be a certain minimum F.Q. that would be required to try-out for the team. People simultaneously weaker, slower and smaller than average would not even be given try-outs. But except for this minimal screening, coaches would not find the F.Q. particularly useful. In fact, coaches would *differentiate* the measures that they use. One might consider developing a number of different kinds of F.Q.'s and calling them P.F.Q.'s (pro football quotients):

P.F.Q.$_1$ (interior linemen)

P.F.Q.$_2$ (running back)

P.F.Q.$_3$ (quarterback)

P.F.Q.$_4$ (line-backers)

P.F.Q.$_5$ (defensive backs and flankers)

P.F.Q.$_6$ (punters and placekickers).

For example, the test for interior linemen (P.F.Q.$_1$) would emphasize size and strength and aggressiveness. Flankers and defensive backs (P.F.Q.$_5$) require speed and ability to change direction quickly. For punting and placekicking (P.F.Q.$_6$), one could consider developing complex tests for strength of leg, coordination, reflex, etc., but it would probably suffice to check how far someone can kick the ball. The ingredients of the P.F.Q.'s thus differ greatly.

In the real world, even with college performance as a try-out and guide, scouts for the various pro teams do try to make measurements such as size, speed, and strength, and then they use comparative charts to help decide who should be drafted. Some teams even give elaborate psychological tests!

Some definite lessons can be drawn from this pro football model:

1. *A simplistic measure of performance is of limited value in determining competence in the real world.* While many pro football players would be good at one-on-one football, the F.Q. is too unspecific to be useful as a selection device. There are different significant measures for different roles.

2. *Some attributes that are needed for success in one area are unnecessary in other areas.* A lineman does not have to see particularly well. (Alex Karras, who leaves his glasses in the locker room, says he plays by Braille.) A quarterback must be durable, but he doesn't need to be very fast. (Sonny Jurgenson, like Bobby Layne, has a classic, rather sedentary beer belly.) A placekicker can be quite small.

3. *Some attributes necessary for success in one area may be incompatible with assets needed in another.* The weight and strength needed by a lineman are so great that it is physically impossible for him to be a flanker or a halfback. Technically this is because strength and speed are different functions of weight.

4. *People with highly varied attributes are needed.* The real world of pro football requires diverse people with different talents. It is a world of specialists.

5. *Test results alone are not particularly useful when choices must be made.* Even with charts and figures, together with performance reports from four years of college play, the teams do not do a good job drafting. Time and again high draft choices are dropped and free agents (people not even drafted) are signed and succeed. Think how scouts would do with only tests to guide them, particularly if only the F.Q. was used.

THE COMPLEXITY OF INTELLIGENCE

The mental abilities needed for coping in the real world are at least as complex as the physical abilities needed in pro football. Scientists, business men, salesmen, accountants, musicians and actors each need different kinds and combinations of mental skills. A creative artist does not need mathematical ability. A scientist does not have to think as quickly as a salesman or an athlete. Further, the complex of mental abilities required to perform successfully as a scientist, say, may be incompatible with those required to be a successful political leader. There is no ideal intelligence.

The relationship of I.Q. to the mental abilities needed in the real world is similar to that of our imaginary F.Q. to the ability to play pro football. There is probably a minimum I.Q. required for good performance in many specialized occupations. But beyond that we can see certain people with low I.Q.'s doing better even in mental tasks than some people with higher I.Q.'s. Success often depends on interest, inclination and training. Moreover, success can depend also on good looks, height, musical ability, persistence, character, and luck.

THE DIFFERENCE BETWEEN I.Q. AND INTELLIGENCE

People with unusual mental capacities are called intelligent by the average man. Psychologists cannot measure such complex capacities, but they *can* measure something that they call I.Q. In the introductions to their papers on the subject, most psychologists state that when they talk about 'intelligence,' they merely mean what I.Q. tests measure—an essentially limited and artificial definition. The papers themselves, however, often give the impression that I.Q. is something more fundamental and significant.

I.Q. *is* about the only relatively stable mental characteristic of children, but it is only a moderately useful measure of mental ability. In its dangerous simplicity, it obscures the richness of mental quality.

RELATION BETWEEN I.Q. AND SUCCESS

I.Q.'s have been measured for a long time and about the only thing we know about I.Q. scores is that, to a major extent, they predict success in school, both in terms of grades and of number of years of school completed. On the average, children with higher I.Q.'s tend to like school, to stay longer and to do better.

Professor Christopher Jencks has summarized well the limited nature of even this kind of predictability:*

* *The New Republic,* September 13, 1969, p. 26.

". . . neither a student's academic achievement nor the number of years of school he completes is *completely* determined by his I.Q. There are all kinds of other things at work, of which family background is the most obvious and personality probably the most important. Taken together, all these have considerably more influence than I.Q. on both academic success and persistence in school. After school the importance of I.Q. diminishes even further.

Jencks' conclusions seem to differ enormously from the Herrnstein's now famous syllogism relating I.Q. and success:

"If differences in mental abilities are inherited, and if success requires these abilities, and if earnings and prestige depend on success, then social standing (which reflects earnings and prestige) will be based to some extent on inherited differences among people."

But in fact, they in many ways point to the same conclusions. In order to show why this is so, we must try to quantify the relationship.

The measurement of the strength of a relationship between two factors is determined by the fraction of the variation in one that is determined by the other. Thus some psychologists have estimated that genetics accounts for 75 percent of the variation in I.Q. in white populations. Now, if I.Q. in turn accounts for, say 75 percent of the variation in mental ability (and if these correlations are independent), then the relationship between genetics and mental ability is determined by multiplying these two percentages, which equals 55%. The following inferences are then also deductible.

"*If differences in mental ability are inherited*": We estimate that this statement describes 55 percent of the variation.

"*If success requires these abilities*": Given the range of occupations and performances deemed successful in America, and the role of luck, and non-mental skills, mental ability might account for 50 percent of the difference in success.

"*If earnings and prestige depend on success*": Success may account for 60 percent of earnings and prestige. Prestige and earnings are often independent of each other (for example, preachers and swindlers).

"Then social standing (which reflects earnings and prestige) will be based (to some extent) on inherited differences among people.": To find out how large the "some extent" is we must multiply the 55 percent in the first proposition, by the 50 percent in the second proposition by the 60 percent in the third proposition, and we find that *social standing (which reflects earnings and prestige) will depend about 15 percent on inherited I.Q. differences among people and therefore about 85 percent on other factors!*

Thus the statements of Professors Jencks and Herrnstein, when examined carefully, actually mean the same thing!

I.Q. AND RACE

All of these factors—the interaction of heredity and environment, the complexity of intelligence compared to the simplicity of the I.Q., and the small relationship between I.Q. and success—would apply if there were no blacks in America.

The one additional factor—and it is the one that has loomed rather large in the present literary/scholarly controversy—is the comparison between blacks and whites in I.Q. but again it is difficult to really define who is black since American blacks have come from a variety of distinct tribal groups and have a certain number of genes from the white population. The Coleman report defined blacks as those people who are looked upon as black by themselves and their neighbors and are treated as black by society. This definition, it should be noted, is a *cultural* and not a genetic one.

It is generally accepted that the mean of black children's I.Q. is about 15 points below that of white children (using the cultural definition rather than the genetic one). Even the hereditarians agree that some of this difference can be attributed to environment, since the average environment for blacks in America is demonstrably worse than that for whites.

We cannot realistically undertake experiments to tell how

much of the mean I.Q. difference between blacks and whites is due to environment,* but we *can* get some idea of what extremes in environment can do to I.Q. In one of the few studies of separated white identical twins, four of the nineteen pairs studied had I.Q. differences greater than 15 points—differences that had to be due to environment. It is reasonable to assume that the different social, economic, and psychological treatment of blacks compared to whites can account for effects just as great.

Heber found in the Milwaukee ghetto that mothers with I.Q.'s below 80 were much more likely to have children with I.Q.'s below 80. Jensen used this observation as one of the arguments for the heritability of I.Q. Recently, Heber took new-born children whose mothers had low I.Q.'s. He intervened heavily in these children's lives with talk, stimulation and toys. His preliminary results indicate that these children after four years get high I.Q. scores. A valid conclusion might be that the *environment* of a very low I.Q. parent can produce a low I.Q. child.

THE PERVASIVENESS OF RACIAL THINKING

Some people justify the different treatment of blacks and whites in our society on the grounds that the I.Q. of blacks is lower. *In fact the average difference between black and white I.Q. is about the same as the average difference between children in the same family.* When this difference occurs in a family, there is little difference in treatment of the children (except perhaps to make an effort to improve conditions for a lower

---

* We would have to bring up a black identical twin as a white, while his twin was brought up as a black, or bring up a white identical twin as a black while *his* twin was brought up as a white. But even this experiment would be in question because the black child always has important aspects of his culture ever present. His treatment by whites, the psychological feeling of oppression, the difference in cultural attitudes toward tests, the differences in upbringing of blacks and whites would indicate that you cannot conclusively tell, nor can you devise realistic experiments to tell, whether the average difference between black and whites is due to heredity or environment.

27

performing child), but when it occurs in our human family and particularly when this difference is associated with skin color, then the difference becomes the subject of lengthy insinuating articles and concern.

Jacques Barzun has studied the 'scientific' work in the study of races in Europe in the nineteenth and twentieth centuries. The problem facing the European anthropologists was how to account for the differences between aristocrats and plebians. There was no *visible* difference—such as skin color—that could be classified as inferior and yet an hereditary aristocracy seemed to require a basis in superior genetic endowment.

With the rise of nationalism, nations as well as classes sought to claim superiority on the grounds of innate differences. There were obviously some differences in hair and skin color between populations in different parts of Europe, but the variety of admixture made these traits a slippery basis for national policy.

Finally, the anthropologists discovered the cephalic index which was determined by dividing the longest diameter of the skull into the shortest diameter and multiplying by 100. The Mediterranean races were held to be the long-headed and the Celts round-headed. From these differences were postulated all kinds of cultural and temperamental differences. Frantic measurements of skulls and heads were made, and long detailed papers were published showing that one sub-group or another was or was not descended from the superior (long-headed) Indo-European invaders that conquered the less able (round-headed) Celts.

Dozens of researchers expanded on this work, culminating in 5,000 measurements on a single skull! Such an effort would be laughable today, but it was taken very seriously at the time and had a significant effect on society's thinking. Barzun quotes Alfred Fouillée who in 1893 said, "Masses of men will be massacring one another for one degree more or less in their cephallic index."

In fact, masses of men were murdered before and during the Second World War, but on the grounds of the mystical Aryan blood rather than head shapes.

Racist thinking obviously fulfills a powerful psychological need to feel that one's group is superior, whether that group is defined by neighborhood, region, sex or ethnic origin. It is too easy for people to forget the fact that the average differences between large groups of people are smaller than the differences among individual members of these groups.

WHAT OF THE FUTURE?

Herrnstein is concerned that we will so equalize the environment that only hereditary differences remain. There will then develop a permanent caste of low I.Q. people. Professor Edward Banfield in *The Unheavenly City* worries about what the decline in death rate among the poor is doing to the cities. Jensen and Shockley are concerned that blacks of low I.Q. are reproducing at more than the average rate and that this will be bad for society.

All these concerns seem to stem from the feeling that genetically determined factors in intelligence and/or success will become more and more important in the future and that culturally determined factors will become less and less important.

These concerns overlook a few things:

1. *It is not clear what genetically related traits society will value in the future.* I.Q. is only moderately valuable now, and we cannot tell whether it will become more or less important. Even today society values other genetically related traits such as height, good looks, and physical strength. In the future we may find that arithmetic ability will be superseded by computers, that more machines and fewer people will be needed to do scientific research, and that we may value athletes and movie stars even more.

2. *Society is adaptable.* The great strength of our society is its ability to adjust to the needs of its citizens. Even if there were to be a gradual decline in I.Q. (for which there is no evidence), our culture can adjust, just as the Army adjusted quite well to illiterates in World War II.

3. *Polygenic traits do not "breed true" in human society.*

29

Variation, not constancy, is the rule in heredity of polygenic traits. There is every reason to believe that some parents of high I.Q. will have some children of low I.Q. and that parents with low I.Q. will have some children with high I.Q. One would expect this as much in the future as in the past.

4. *Mobility is related more to cultural than to genetic factors.* J. B. S. Haldane, the great British geneticist, moved to India, late in life, to study the caste system, because he felt India provided a unique chance to observe the effects of population segregation that had occurred over centuries. In one of his last speeches, Haldane pointed out that although the early segregation of the higher castes could have been due to genetic factors, these castes could have retained their genetic superiority only by following the animal breeders' practice of culling out genetically inferior members. In fact, the Indian castes did *not* cull out their less gifted children either through killing them or disinheriting them. Similarly, in our society, the rich and powerful use their advantages to try to *overcome* their offsprings' handicaps, and to some parents that is precisely the most important reason for wealth and power. Thus, we see middle class parents trying hard to get their less able children into good colleges, small business men taking their sons into the business, union men trying to limit membership in apprenticeship programs to their sons and nephews. This tendency is not unique to capitalist society. It exists in socialist societies (see Solzhenitzyn's accounts), and in primitive societies as well.

In looking toward the future, we must try to eliminate racial thinking. The racial problem in our society is not that blacks have lower I.Q. than whites, it is that we do not treat blacks equally. We must treat people as individuals, and not according to the average I.Q. of their group.

Social scientists are working to improve their inadequate understanding of how society works. But their tools are limited and, at least in the case of I.Q., not sophisticated enough to be useful in drawing conclusions about the way the world really works or should work.

3

WHAT COLOR IS I.Q.?
INTELLIGENCE AND RACE

BY CHRISTOPHER JENCKS

"There is an increasing realization among students of the psychology of the disadvantaged that the discrepancy in their average performance cannot be completely or directly attributed to discrimination or inequalities in education. It seems not unreasonable, in view of the fact that intelligence variation has a large genetic component, to hypothesize that genetic factors may play a part in this picture. But such an hypothesis is anathema to many social scientists. The idea that the lower average intelligence and scholastic performance of Negroes could involve not only environmental but also genetic factors had indeed been strongly denounced. But it has been neither contradicted nor discredited by evidence."

Had an article expressing this view appeared in a technical journal, or at a time when liberal ideas were less on the defensive, or under the name of a Southern segregationist, it would probably have passed unnoticed. But it appeared in the winter, 1969, *Harvard Educational Review*, under the name of Arthur Jensen, one of the nation's leading educational psychologists, at a time when liberal ideas about the causes and cures of racism were badly discredited. So "How Much Can We Boost I.Q. and Schola;tic Achievement?" has been trumpeted around the world by *Time, Newsweek, U.S. News* and *World Report, The New York Times,* and a dozen syndicated columnists, has been discussed at a Cabinet meeting, and has made its author the most publicized (and vilified) figure in psychology today.

Jensen makes at least four distinct arguments. First, the author asserts that compensatory education for disadvantaged children has failed to increase their I.Q. scores. Second, he argues that children with low I.Q.'s tend to be genetically as well as environmentally handicapped, and that efforts to raise their I.Q.'s by improving the school environment are consequently misguided. Third, he argues that genes play a major role not just in I.Q. differences among individuals from the same ethnic or socioeconomic group, but also in I.Q. differences between such groups. Fourth, he concludes that we can nonetheless teach the Three R.'s to low-I.Q. children if we place less emphasis on the manipulation of abstractions and more emphasis on rote learning. Jensen presents the first and last of these arguments very sketchily, and I will not try to deal with them here. The bulk of his article is devoted to his second argument, that is, that individuals with low I.Q.'s typically differ genetically from those with high I.Q.'s, and it is the clearest exposition of this subject ever published. Jensen's critics, who replied in the Spring issue of the *Harvard Educational Review,* offer no persuasive evidence against his position. Jensen's most controversial claim is, however, his third argument, that is, that I.Q. differences between groups also have a genetic component. Here he is far from persuasive—though neither, I regret to say, are his critics.

The idea that biological differences between individuals affect their intelligence is hardly new. The pioneers of the mental testing movement in America believed men were born different, and they set out to develop tests that would measure those differences. While their efforts were not wholly successful, neither were they a complete flop. They created a variety of mental tests whose results, while clearly influenced by individual experience, also showed a strong independent relationship to heredity. The tests whose results proved to be most influenced by heredity and least by environment were individually administered I.Q. tests, such as the Stanford-Binet.

There has been a great deal of debate about whether these I.Q. tests really measure "intelligence." Some critics maintain that they measure only one aspect of intelligence, which psychologists happen to think important because they have a lot of it. Others maintain that the tests measure only familiarity with middle-class culture. Psychologists usually sidestep the question by defining "intelligence" as "whatever I.Q. tests measure," which is a bit confusing since 99 percent of the population continues to use the word "intelligence" in a different way. It seems safer to say merely that I.Q. tests measure I.Q., whatever that may be, and then to investigate whether people with high I.Q.'s differ in any important way from people with low I.Q.'s.

Critics of I.Q. testing argue that there is no way to determine whether I.Q. is intrinsically important. American children are given I.Q. tests, American adults are impressed (or depressed) by the results, and children are treated accordingly. This means that a high I.Q. score, like a white skin, will be an asset even if I.Q. itself is no more intrinsically important than skin color. This argument can, however, easily be overdone. Many elementary schools, for example, use I.Q. tests to assign pupils to different classrooms and curricula, and this may encourage low—I.Q. pupils to become poor readers and help high-I.Q. pupils become good readers. But there are also plenty of elementary schools which do *not* segregate high and low I.Q. pupils. I.Q. scores predict academic achievement with moderate accuracy in these schools too. Indeed, I.Q. predicts achievement moderately well even in schools which do not give I.Q. tests. Similarly, some high schools and many colleges today choose among applicants on the basis of group "aptitude" tests (like the College Board's famous SAT) which measure something like I.Q. But even in 1918, before schools and colleges employed such tests, the Army found an extremely high correlation between men's scores on a group aptitude test and the number of years of schooling the men had completed. These relationships between I.Q. and academic success are almost as strong among blacks as among whites. So while I.Q. testing may be partly a matter of self-fulfilling prophecies, it is not just that.

33

On the other hand, neither a student's academic achievement nor the number of years of school he completes is *completely* determined by his I.Q. There are all kinds of other things at work, of which family background is the most obvious and personality probably the most important. Taken together, these "non-cognitive" factors have considerably more influence than I.Q. on both academic success and persistence in school.) After school the importance of I.Q. diminishes even further. Men's I.Q.'s account for only about a fifth of the variation in their occupational status and a tenth of the variation in their incomes. These relationships are even weaker among blacks. The relationship between I.Q. and adult success results, moreover, largely from the fact that I.Q. is strongly related to the amount of schooling a man completes. Among men with the same amount of schooling, those with high I.Q.'s are hardly more successful than those with low I.Q.'s.

I.Q. also seems to play a role in mating. There are, it is true, some American subcultures in which people choose their mates on the basis of things like height, sex appeal, personality, and money, ignoring I.Q. When this happens, the demographers say there is no "assortative mating" by I.Q. In such a subculture the typical wife will have a husband with an I.Q. of 100 (the national average) no matter what her own I.Q. In other American subcultures, however, the marriage market is closely tied to colleges and universities and there is a great deal of assortative mating by I.Q. This means that a woman with a high I.Q. is likely to have a husband whose I.Q. is well above average, and vice versa.

Taking America as a whole, it seems that the typical white woman marries somebody whose I.Q. is about halfway between her own and the national average. A woman with an I.Q. of 116, for example, typically marries a man with an I.Q. of about 108. At first glance this may seem to imply that a man with an I.Q. of 108 typically marries a woman with an I.Q. of 116, but that is not the case. The typical man with an I.Q. of 108 ends up with a wife whose I.Q. is about 104. In this respect

34

the sexes are of necessity equal. Whether these patterns are found among black as well as white Americans nobody seems to know.

People with low I.Q.'s are less likely to marry or have children than people with high I.Q.'s. But once people with low I.Q.'s have had one child they tend to have more than other people. The result is that fertility and I.Q. end up almost uncorrelated, at least in contemporary white America. Nobody knows, however, whether this has always been true. Nor does anybody know if it is true among blacks.

In brief, despite the conscious and unconscious biases influencing the construction of I.Q. tests, they appear to measure something of moderate importance. I stress the word "moderate." The evidence does not suggest that I.Q. is as important as those who live by shuffling paper usually assume.

The next question is whether variations in I.Q. result primarily from variations in the environment to which people have been exposed, or whether they result from genetically determined differences in the way people respond to their environment. In trying to answer this question we have to remember that neither Jensen nor any other contemporary scholar claims that environment *can't* affect I.Q. scores. Children are not born putting round pegs in round holes and square pegs in square holes; they learn from experience. If the environment does not offer a child the chance to learn something, he doesn't learn it. This means it is easy to imagine (or even to create) environments in which no child, regardless of genetic potential, develops the knowledge or skills needed to do well on an I.Q. test. Jensen merely asserts that such environments are quite rare in modern America. As he sees it, most children have about the same opportunity to learn the things they need to know to do well on tests like the Stanford-Binet. So far as the development of I.Q. is concerned, Jensen thinks equality of opportunity is already a near reality. If he is correct it follows that differences in I.Q. score must reflect genetically determined differences in the way people respond to their environment.

Jensen offers a variety of evidence for believing that I.Q. differences derive primarily from genetic differences, but two facts are especially relevant.

(1) Children reared in the same home tend to have very different I.Q. scores. This is particularly true of unrelated children, who have no genes in common. If you take random pairs of unrelated 10-year-olds, for instance, you can expect their mental ages to differ by an average of about twenty months. If you take random pairs of unrelated 10-year-olds who have shared the same home since the age of 6 months or less, their mental ages will still differ by an average of about 17 months. In the language of statistics, we can say that sharing the same home environment after the age of 6 months accounts for only 20–30 percent of the variation in unrelated children's I.Q. scores.

(2) Identical twins, who have all their genes in common, have quite similar I.Q. scores. This is true even when they are raised in different families and different social classes from the age of six months or less. Instead of mental ages that differ by an average of 20 months, these twins can be expected to show mean differences of only 7 to 10 months. Common genes, in other words, seem to account for 75–85 percent of the variation in such twins' I.Q. scores.

Studies such as these are not definitive. For one thing, they do not allow us to distinguish between the effect of inheritance and the effect of prenatal and early postnatal environments. There is strong evidence, however, that identical twins' prenatal environments are far from identical. Identical twins' birth weights, for example, differ more than do birth weights of nonidentical twins. Yet identical twins' I.Q.'s differ much less than nonidentical twins. And nonidentical twins, who should be made more alike by similar prenatal environments, are little more alike than siblings of differing age and sex. All this suggests that prenatal environments, while clearly important in certain cases, aren't a very good explanation for most variations in I.Q.

A more serious objection to these studies is that they cover very few children. There has been hardly any serious research along these lines in America for a generation. This would be understandable if all the early studies had been in agreement, but they were not. Different investigators measured I.Q. in different ways. The range of environmental variation was different in some studies than in others. Indeed, some of the best studies were done in England, not America. Different investigators reach different conclusions. Nonetheless, I do not think anyone could read through the enormous body of research on these problems and still believe that genes have *no* effect on I.Q.

A precise estimate of the relative importance of heredity and environment in the development of I.Q. is almost certain to be wrong and is likely to be misleading. Jensen makes a number of simplifying assumptions and concludes that in contemporary white America environmental variations account for only a fifth of the variation in individual I.Q. scores, while genetic differences account for the other four-fifths. This estimate strikes me as high; my guess is that environment accounts for closer to a third than a fifth of the variation in white America I.Q.'s. The critical point, however, is not the precise figure but the order of magnitude. Jensen is very likely correct in arguing that among white Americans the range of environmental variation is small enough so that it accounts for less of the total variation in I.Q. than genes.

The foregoing paragraph must be read carefully. It refers to I.Q., not academic achievement, and it refers to white America, not all America. Jensen's own argument suggests that environment apparently has more influence on academic achievement than on I.Q. More important, studies of children who are not reared by their natural parents can only tell us about the effects of environmental differences within groups whose parents adopt one another's children. We obviously have no studies of identical twins reared apart, in which one twin was black and reared in a black family while the other twin was white and reared in a white family. We do not even have any studies of unrelated children reared together in which one child was

37

black and the other white. And if we did have such studies, we would nonetheless have to question whether such children's environments were really similar.

Adoption studies, then, tell us a lot about individual differences within a given group but very little about differences between groups. Still, the usual reason for believing in genetic differences between races is that (a) "I.Q. is mainly determined by genes," and (b) "the I.Q. differences between races are very large." The first of these propositions is, as Jensen himself demonstrates very elegantly, an oversimplification. The second proposition is true but irrelevant. The typical black American scores below 80–90 percent of his white age-mates on virtually any test requiring abstract reasoning, be it verbal or nonverbal, "culture free" or "culture bound," "aptitude" or "achievement." This has been so since black-white differences in test performance were first measured during World War I. It is true at all ages above six. It is not true on certain tests commonly given before the age of six, but these early tests do not seem to measure the same thing as later I.Q. tests.

The fact that black-white I.Q. differences are large does not prove, however, that they are genetic in origin. The average white I.Q. is 100, while the black average is about 85. Something like a sixth of white identical twins reared apart show comparable differences. These differences are due to environment, since identical twins always have the same genes. If a sixth of the white families rearing these twins differed enough to produce a 15-point I.Q. difference, it is surely conceivable that the typical white home and neighborhood also differs from the typical black home and neighborhood enough to produce such a difference.

Jensen makes a great deal of the fact that black children do worse on I.Q. and achievement tests, and are six times more likely to be mentally retarded, than white children at the same socio-economic level. But what does this prove? The fact that a black and a white child both have fathers who do the same kind of work or mothers who spent the same number of years in school does not mean the two children are treated the same

38

way, either at home or elsewhere. Jewish children also do better on I.Q. tests than Christians at the same socio-economic level, but very few people conclude that Jews are genetically superior to Christians. Instead, we conclude that Jews treat their children differently from Christians even when their occupations, incomes and education are the same.

This same line of reasoning also applies to Jensen's comparison of Negroes to American Indians. Indian children are much worse off economically than Negro children. Yet Indian children seem to do substantially better than Negroes on tests of academic competence. If socio-economic status were the only environmental factor affecting academic performance, we would have to conclude that Indians had a genetic advantage over Negroes which offset their environmental disadvantage. But since the available evidence suggests that socio-economic status is not the most important environmental factor influencing test scores, inferences about Negro-Indian genetic differences seem unwarranted.

If social and economic status is not the critical environmental factor influencing I.Q., what is? There is evidence that conditions in the womb may be important. Jensen reports, however, that prenatal deprivation usually leads to poor performance on infant tests of physical coordination and development. Hence if large numbers of black babies suffered serious prenatal deprivation, we would expect them to do worse than whites on early tests of coordination and physical skills. They don't; in fact, they often do better. A committed environmentalist might argue that black babies' prenatal environments, while adequate for the early development of motor skills, stunt those parts of the brain which affect later capacity for abstract thinking. This theory seems rather far-fetched, however. While a significant number of black children may well suffer serious prenatal damage, Jensen's evidence suggests that we should probably look elsewhere to explain racial differences in I.Q. scores. But it hardly follows that we must look to genes. We might do equally well to look at patterns of child rearing.

Jensen's most plausible reason for believing in the existence of genetic differences between races is that fertility patterns among blacks are different from those among whites. Poorly educated black women *who marry* have more children than well-educated white women who marry. Well-educated white women who marry have more children than well-educated black women who marry. If (1) this difference holds when you include women who do not marry, and if (2) well-educated blacks are also high I.Q. blacks, and if (3) high I.Q. blacks are also genetically advantaged blacks and if (4) racial differences in fertility patterns are of long standing rather than of recent origin, and if (5) these differences have not been offset by other tendencies working in the opposite direction, there must now be appreciable genetic differences between the typical black and the typical white. But all those "ifs" call for careful scrutiny, which they have not received from Jensen or anyone else.

Black men with high scores on the Armed Forces Qualification Test have usually had a lot more education than black men with low scores. This test is fairly well correlated with I.Q. It is perfectly conceivable, however, that the same environmental advantages which lead to high educational attainment also lead to a high AFQT score, and that the genes which influence these scores do not influence how long a black man stays in school. Furthermore, the association between I.Q. and persistence in school only shows up among the better educated. This suggests that the association may have been a by-product of the expansion of educational opportunity as blacks moved off plantations. It is rash to suppose that present differences in fertility between highly educated and poorly educated blacks indicate long-standing fertility differences between high and low I.Q. blacks. On the contrary while it seems clear there is no significant relationship between I.Q. and fertility among contemporary white women, there is reason to suppose there may have been a negative relationship earlier in the industrial revolution. If so, it could be *whites* who are genetically disadvantaged.

None of this proves that blacks and whites are genetically indistinguishable. On the contrary, they are genetically different in a number of respects, of which skin color is only the most obvious. Furthermore, anybody who ponders the problem is likely to conclude that if two ethnic groups have different gene pools with respect to skin color, facial features, and so forth, they could also have different gene pools with respect to I.Q. But all kinds of things *could* be true, whereas only a few *are* true.

Were there a dispassionate observer, who could look at these arguments without political or personal bias, I think he would conclude that neither Jensen nor his critics had offered a persuasive explanation of I.Q. differences between blacks and whites. He would probably also conclude that neither geneticists nor social scientists know enough about the determinants of I.Q. scores to design a study which would fully resolve our present confusion. Nonetheless, Jensen's decision to reopen this ancient controversy without first gathering more evidence strikes me as a serious political blunder.

Still, the topic *has* been reopened. This being so, it is important to keep reminding ourselves of a point I made at the outset: I.Q., whatever its origin, plays a relatively modest role in determining a man's life chances. Even if I.Q. differences between blacks and whites have a genetic as well as an environmental basis, such differences have very little to do with the way blacks and whites are treated in contemporary America. Otis Dudley Duncan has shown, for example, that blacks with high I.Q.'s are almost as disadvantaged economically as those with low I.Q.'s. They are also disadvantaged in almost every other respect, from their dealings with the police to their dealings with landlords. Low I.Q.'s are not the cause of America's racial problems and higher I.Q.'s would not solve these problems. Any white reader who doubts this should simply ask himself whether he would trade the genes which make his skin white for genes which would raise his I.Q. 15 points.

4

SPEED AND DIRECTION

The question of I.Q. heredity has social importance because as with all human traits, the control and predictability of human behavior, rather than some ideal of knowledge, is our objective. On the one hand we conjure visions of a mad psychometrician shunting people into life-time social positions on the basis of their I.Q. scores. On the other we resent being manipulated by conditions beyond our control. The hereditarian view is that we can do very little to improve our genetic inheritance and that genes rule the structure of human society. Leaving aside the question as to the meaning of "improve," this is not a particularly challenging social prediction. History has been quite negative on the comparative group advantages of a high average I.Q. As a group, for instance, Jews have (so far as we can determine) always had a higher average I.Q. as compared to Christians. But this neither helped the Jews of Nazi Germany, nor Jews in Europe as a whole during the last two thousand years of sporadic pogroms. At any rate there are more cogent arguments than the history of the Jews for believing that the I.Q. is not as socially important as the hereditarians claim. Is there, then, a difference between the meaning of I.Q. and intelligence?

THE REAL MEANING OF I.Q.

Confronted with the problem of defining intelligence as something real, psychometricians have chosen to define I.Q. intelligence as what I.Q. test measures.[1] This reverses the normal procedure in science which is to define a subject matter before measuring it. The conceptual definition of I.Q. presently resembles one that would make the value of money depend only on the paper amount printed. Inflated money, however, does not quite mean what its amount reads. Yet let us accept for the moment the I.Q. definition above. Does an I.Q. *reflect* a real learning ability? I would say yes, a particular kind of ability. An I.Q. for most people can indicate how well they will perform in situations with demands similar to those required on an I.Q. test. Of course, there are no identical situations to an I.Q. test in reality, as even the hereditarians agree that academic performance is definitely subject to variables of the learning environment. For Jensen and other hereditarians the major problem of psychometric science is still the absence of a subject matter,[2] which is undoubtedly why he writes wistfully of psychologists some day discovering "atoms of memory."[3] But a correlation of high I.Q.'s with professional occupations (status jobs) can work two ways, it being possible to argue with equal force that either the I.Q. is dependent on class, or the reverse. There is, either way, no material form of intelligence in biological terms. Definitely the test performance is real, but the rest is reasoning and an infinite number of arguments. Moreover, one can even validly dispute whether measurements in themselves constitute a science. No one knows what the conditions are that determine I.Q. correlations with a particular job status.

Although most psychologists have been unsatisfied with measurements alone, the lack of material evidence for a genetic explanation of I.Q. scores is the reason for the present controversy. No one criticizes Jensen for wanting "intelligence atoms" and a higher average I.Q. through controlled human breeding. But he reasons from concepts of science fiction.

What does an I.Q. mean? It is the rate at which a person performs on an I.Q. test, an "intelligence quotient" according to prescribed rules and in comparison to other persons of the same standard age. Only that, whatever its lesser or greater coincidence to height, toe nail thickness, or skin color.

To avoid the implications of speed in I.Q. scores the innovators of I.Q. tried to create a distinction between so-called speed and power tests.[4] Why? In examining test results psychologists discovered that chance could play a large part in determining a person's score. For example, a high score could be achieved simply by attempting as many test items as possible. When there was never enough time to complete the test and, if one was not marked down for wrong guesses, one naturally benefited from any correct guesses. There was always a good chance of getting a correct answer on the multiple choice, with one's odds determined by the number of choices. To eliminate or reduce the element of chance (which psychologists called "speed") some tests were constructed so that everyone could complete the test. This simple change in testing method led psychologists to believe that they finally had a measure of thinking power. The reasoning was that the scores from completed tests indicated more deliberation in the pupil's response to questions. Then, even if the pupil guessed, he was thinking more about the choice of guesses because of the added time. Yet despite the subtle statistical procedures for estimating the proportion of "speed" and the so-called "power" (the real intelligence for the testers), the distinction between a score based on speed and one supposedly based on power was just an arbitrary way of scoring rather than an absolute difference in testing. For psychologists today a "speed" test (one with scores heavily susceptible to random guessing) depends upon the number of test items completed rather than the correct completions; whether right or wrong the number of attempted items add to the total of a person's score. The power test differs only in that the number of correct items is a total from which incorrect attempts have been subtracted.[5] Put another way, in the "speed" test one is only rewarded for correct answers; in the "power" test one is punished for incorrect answers. But both tests define the field of activity and limit the time in which one may take the test. As a performance rate, the I.Q. is still a speed of defined action.

This means that the more significant part of an I.Q. score (rank among chronological peers being the other part) is exactly as the raw test score for any number of scholastic tests, where an achievement test result in, say, Math or Chemistry, would mean a level of proficiency only in Math or Chemistry. No one would rationally equate the proficiency level in one scholastic exam with an identical numerical level from another.

What of the high correlation between academic grades and a high I.Q.? The correlation in no way means that an academic learning ability *depends* upon I.Q. test taking ability. Moreover there are substantial reasons why an I.Q. depends upon academic kinds of mental stimulation. Our ability to use abstract languages—or, as psychologists collectively name it, the abstract thinking ability—cannot develop without cultural learning. People learn the words or symbols for indicating real things before they comprehend the symbols as categories, things in the abstract. A developing infant, for example, will first indicate food and other things indifferently as the signals that it has learned for its mother. Later the infant learns distinct symbols for different things but until then it has no way to express differences, or what it knows, because even simple expressions cannot yet be learned. Dr. Heber in the famous Milwaukee Project[6] demonstrated that exposing a child at an early age to a variety of functional things and intensive mental stimulation increases learning rate. Relating this to average I.Q. differences, it is clear that the ease with which we know things enables us to know more about them.

FLUENCY

Since people learn to think abstractly by abstracting the symbols for real things, a hypothetical essence of intelligence (which psychologists call "general ability") would still develop from social experience. An I.Q. range in this regard can certainly be deemed hereditary. Yet there are many people with high I.Q.s who are mediocre students as well as social failures. And the most egregious example of the latter are the computing prodigies who have been unteachable illiterates.[7] Even these "idiot savants," however, had to learn to recognize the symbols that they used to count. So the heredity of the I.Q. means only one thing: the range of potential for improvement in raising one's I.Q. But for normal people that range is quite vast, it being possible to raise a mediocre I.Q. to the so-called genius range. Psychologists will correctly argue that coaching an I.Q. doesn't make the person smarter in learning Swahili.

How could it? The I.Q. tests form a different language. Everyone admits, however, that proficiency in scholastic subjects or a native language would affect an I.Q. And this is because a "logical system" is learned with the acquisition of disciplined knowledge or language. Indeed when the test items are abstract enough they constitute a test of logic. In other words, learning the language of I.Q. tests is no different from learning any other language. Practice increases our learning rate. As we develop our vocabulary—our familiarity with the forms of expression—so we learn to indicate larger meanings in fewer symbols. Thus, in actual fact all disciplined forms of knowledge proceed to mathematization, with terminologies that become more succinct. And this is why a high I.Q. will correlate strongly with length of academic training and high scholastic grades.

THE IMPORTANCE OF CULTURE: WHY THERE CAN BE NO THINKING UNLESS THERE IS SOMETHING THOUGHT

Not so long ago many psychologists would call I.Q. tests "culture free" and barely a fraction ever questioned how "culture free" an academic level or occupational category could be. Most accepted that I.Q. determined who entered certain occupations and made good grades. But today only the hereditarians still believe in the potency of I.Q. as a culture free intelligence. And no one has ever found a "culture free" social success. All of the feral individuals—those wolf children who were discovered in cultural isolation—have either been mentally undeveloped, or have perished after a short time in human society. In all of the reported cases[8] there was a medical basis for determining mental retardation, a condition observed from specific social malfunctioning rather than an I.Q. level. None of these children were ever found to possess a human language and few learned to speak in any but the most child-like language. What must be noted here is that the ability to communicate is the only gauge of intelligence. But disregarding the evidence from studies on the importance of a cultural basis for learning, so-called "culture free" and, later, "culture fair" tests (as the current I.Q. tests are labeled) were constructed, mass produced in one culture and sold to educators for the purpose of sorting a variety of people into professional and non-professional training programs. The wrongness of this policy was, firstly, that it was educationally unsound. The second problem was that the people subjected to I.Q. tests were of different cultures.[9]

The dream of hereditarians to eliminate all cultural bias in I.Q. scores originated from a confused preconception that *culture is superfluous to learning to succeed within cultures*. It was a notion without experimental validity. On the other hand, to have claimed that the I.Q. test, as it stood, was already culturally fair (because people could dramatically improve their competency in any subject but not so much in I.Q. level) would have reduced the meaning of the I.Q. test to that of a maze puzzle, or mental game. This view would have certainly settled the mystery as to why many people with high I.Q.'s find academic subjects difficult, or seem unable to learn in school. Just as we recognize a biological basis for chess champions and computing freaks, so we should accept that there is a special ability for taking tests. This fact can be demonstrated in a very simple way. Take any random statistical group of people and coach them to score high on I.Q. tests. (Or, as was done in the Milwaukee Project, give them prolonged and intensive training in basic academic subjects.) Eventually champions will emerge— that is, two highest scoring persons whose only claim to public attention would be their ability to score the highest I.Q.s. This is confirmed in an easier way if we try to identify social status from the high scoring range in an I.Q. population. It can't be done. There are as many failures as successes with high I.Q.s.

And the larger our test population the truer this is. From either experiment we could conclude that raising one's I.Q. alone would not give one any special advantage for subjects which one has never studied.

Despite what the hereditarians say (see the exchange between Professor Herrnstein and myself, *The Atlantic*, Dec. 1971 and Feb. 1972) nothing changes the fact that the direction of learning (and performing) determines any amount of what people achieve. This is the only way that we can logically explain the difference in achievements of two peoples having identical measured abilities. And here the hereditarians lose on their own terms. For example, much has been made of the fact that American Indians and whites have similar average I.Q.s above the average for American blacks. And from the tests that show these results a case is made for considering the tests as culturally fair to blacks, it then following that black test scores are genetically inferior and blacks are inferior persons. . . . The best response to this argument is simply to observe that for all the good it has done the Indians, Indian-white I.Q. averages have been true since Columbus. Achievement is in terms of the result, which is to say that our skills must be as diverse as the symbols in which they are expressed, human energy and imagination having an infinite number of points to apply themselves. Both skills and language develop through our imagination and, irreducibly, both mean more symbols. Really symbols are just paper and ink. And difference being form, meaning comes from the unique twists in the same black line. Intelligence, in short, is not reducible to "g" or anything else, except in a plural, categorical sense, as the intelligence data, or controversy. So the correlation of job proficiency to test aptitudes—the ratio—is still an expression of two kinds of skill.

This dichotomy further divides by the fact that there are always those who only do well in theory and others who only prove themselves in actual application; book soldiers, thirty-day wonders, on the one hand and self-made men on the other. Any predictions from test results to later success in life (one life, that is, not the saga of a chosen people) are fifty-fifty, or purely coincidental, for either the book soldiers or the self-made men. Those who fall into neither category achieve according to the kind of comparisons made against them.

But in equitable political systems the decision as to who should have professional training ought to rest on the person's performance in the training. Liking to do something—when one actually does it—is the best aptitude. By excluding a person from higher learning on the basis of a mediocre I.Q. score, present educational policy has assumed that one inherited not so much intelligence as opportunity. The injustice of this policy—which is very popular in the United States and England—is that prolonged actual learning experience could raise the mediocre I.Q.

Now the weakness in most criticism of the hereditary theory of I.Q. has been that most of the critics assumed, as the hereditarians, that an I.Q. determines—because it correlates with—occupational and professional status. Unfortunately this criticism is restricted to the percentage of genetic influence in an I.Q. score. It ignores the more important problem of how social factors have always limited our hereditary nature. As Jensen observed,[10] an I.Q. is a definite function of a human genetic structure, so it is obvious sophistry to debate a choice between an I.Q. determined wholly by heredity or environment. But having said this, Jensen is oddly unwilling to take the next step. Namely, even accepting that some part—even an 80% part—of our learning speed is hereditary, none of the occupational categories in which our speed is ever demonstrated can be inherited. Furthermore, an 80% hereditary I.Q. would not mean that 80% of our hereditary learning speed was involved in academic performance. Of course when it was thought that black children were becoming less intelligent with school years (as measured by I.Q. tests) the hereditarians explained this curious variance as an indication that compensatory education programs were a failure. Overlooked was the fact that genetic I.Q. scores should

49

not have varied so much as they did if they were 80% genetically determined. One could have all along raised the slum child's I.Q. by coaching him on taking the test. But since boosting a person's I.Q. doesn't give him a better job, or any particularly useful knowledge, what would be the point? Except on the I.Q. test, a coached I.Q. alone will not even make a person any smarter. Human genetic structure is the biological condition for the social freedom that people have in shaping their culture. This is the only plausible view inasmuch as the most stable I.Q. scores are obtained from tests having fewest items unique to a culture.

So the hereditarians have a point. As we know, selective mating has produced predictable physical adaptations in animals. For instance, it is possible to breed maze-learning proficiency in rats.[11] But here we come full circle back to idiot savants.[12] The maze is just a game. Undoubtedly people could be bred for predictable I.Q. scores on a so-called "culture fair" test since that test is essentially a collection of complicated maze puzzles. The point is that "culture fair" things are unreal and people are not just more complex kinds of rats. They either quickly tire of using their abilities for "cultural fair" ends (called doing something for nothing), or they resent being forced to play an endless game.

And of course a "culture fair" person, strictly defined, is not a person at all. It is an animal, or like the wolf-children, a brutalised sub-man unable to communicate with his world except in terms of his appetites.

Inasmuch as a natural species language does not exist, despite the psychological invention called "g" (general learning ability), there can be no thinking unless one has learned a formed way of thinking, or thoughts. To paraphrase Marshall McLuhan, a specific cultural form is the only medium of our messages, human intelligence being the use of intelligible symbols.

RECENT ERRORS IN THE HEREDITARIAN ARGUMENTS

In his controversial *Atlantic Monthly* article, "I.Q.," Harvard Professor Richard Herrnstein misled many readers into believing that standard measures for physical ability and I.Q. could not be compared. Herrnstein wrote that, "Unlike inches, pounds, or seconds, the I.Q. is entirely a measure of relative standing in a given group. No such relationship is tolerated for the conventional measures."[13] The fallacy in this statement is that if an I.Q. was "entirely a measure of relative standing in a given group" it would be an entirely arbitrary figure. As Herrnstein should know, the I.Q. is determined as a ratio of a raw test score and chronological age group. The "relative standing" that an I.Q. signifies is relative to the magnitudes of those two conventional measures. If anyone cared to do it, they could compute quotients for track and field events, the analogy given by Professor Jensen in attempting to explain what an I.Q. meant.[14]

The hereditarians admit that to "coach"[15] a person's I.Q. would invalidate the psychological meaning of his score, an admission which removes any reason to argue that an I.Q. cannot be raised. To coach what Jensen conceives as a "physical ability quotient" would produce identical possibilities and limitations as for I.Q. There would be large variations for individuals and smaller variations for groups. Any change would depend largely on environmental stimulation, that is, exercise. This variation would not be unexpected, for as the hereditarians concede, there is a drastic drop in I.Q. with increasing age after maturity. The average "culture fair" I.Q. may diminish by as much as three-fourths.[16] This must be kept in mind because some hereditarians seriously claim that a person's I.Q. is as stable as his height.[17]

THORNDIKE'S SPURIOUS LEGACY: THE MERITOCRACY

On the basis of a limited nineteenth century European education, E. L. Thorndike (one of the earliest theorists of a genetic interpretation of I.Q.) observed: "In the actual race of life, which is not to get ahead, but to get ahead of somebody, the chief determining factor is heredity."[18] This pitiful logic has ever since been the basis[19] for presuming that a person's I.Q. determines his later social success. Few of Thorndike's proteges have perceived that the philosophy behind the test only works if we can assume that everyone has the same goal. Achievements in different kinds of races cannot be compared.

Thorndike's erroneous dictum leads directly to Herrnstein's prediction that the social order in the United States is developing into an I.Q. ranking system. "Artificial" (as Herrnstein calls social discrimination) barriers will be eliminated and society will become stratified into hereditary castes of ability.[20] That is, people with high I.Q.s will perpetuate a ruling elite. So the "meritocracy" is life once again reduced to a "culture fair" test. Herrnstein, following Thorndike, has singularized the races of life, the only way to realize this dream, and reduced man to a prisoner of his organic inclinations. Life, in other words, is made to resemble a rat's learning maze with a master psychologist (Herrnstein doesn't mean God) working the stimulus-response bell and putting all the winners of his rat race on the same team. Rather poetically, the psychologist has conceived of a competition where the naturally determined winners are only competing against people who never had a chance to win.

Finally, without ridiculing Herrnstein's intentions, it should be pointed out that while nature moves according to mathematical laws, the identity of what moves can never be induced from such laws. The hereditarian mistake was that from the mathematical model of controlled behavior of rats they *induced* that people naturally moved the same way. It was a logical induction as true as 2 and 2 equals 4, and just as vague. With measurements alone we are left to the mercy of our inferences. Scientific data must still be obtained from measured experimentation.

The first lesson from the fallacy of I.Q. is that I.Q. tests should be relegated to their proper status as parlor games where they were first inspired. Parents and educators can help to accomplish this by insisting that academic rank be determined solely from proficiency in what students are required to learn. Previously indirect methods of grading as with the I.Q. begged the question of grading for whom. In any democratic state education should serve the people's needs as individuals, not the military, or industrial goals of a ruling elite.

NOTES

(1) Jensen, Arthur, "How Much Can We Boost I.Q. and Scholastic Achievement?" *Harvard Educational Review,* Winter, 1969, V. 39, N. 1, p. 8.

(2) Jensen, A. *Ibid.*

(3) Jensen, A. *Ibid.* p. 11.

(4) Gulliksen, H., *Theory of Mental Tests,* John Wiley & Sons, N.Y. 1950, pp. 230–231: for more detailed presentations, see: Anastasi, A. and Drake, J. "An empirical comparison of certain techniques for estimating the reliability of speeded tests." *Educational and Psychological Measurement,* 1954, 14, pp. 529–540: Cronbach, L. J. Warrington, W. J., "Time Limit Tests: Estimating their reliability and degree of speeding." *Psychometrika,* 1951, *16,* 167–188.

(5) Gulliksen, H., et. al. *Ibid.*

(6) Strickland, Stephen, "Can Slum Children Learn?" *American Education,* July, 1971.

(7) Ball, W. W. Rouse, "Calculating Prodigies," *The World of Mathematics,* ed. John R. Newman, Simon & Schuster, 1956, v. 1, pp. 465–488.

(8) Gesell, Arnold, *Wolf Child and Human Child,* Harper & Row Broas., N.Y., 1940; Itard, Jean, *The Wild Boy of Aveyron,* N.Y., 1932; Mowry, Robert & Singh, J.A.L., *Wolf Children and Fedral Man,* Harper & Bros., N.Y., 1942 (This is the best work of the three.)

(9) Jensen notes that average (culture fair) I.Q. test scores for Afro-Americans are lower than similar test score averages for American Indians and Spanish speaking Americans. He uncritically accepts this as added proof that I.Q. is mostly geneti-

cally determined, since the social environment of Afro-Americans is often deemed "better" than that for the other two groups. Aside from failing to define all of the social environmental factors so as to make these comparisons valid, Jensen ignores the structural disparity of culture and social mores between an essentially racial group and what are essentially two ethnic-linguistic groups. The latter have a basis for cultural stimulation, whereas a *racial* minority is, as American blacks so often despair, bereft of a distinct culture. The Afro-American group is in fact primarily a racial one because of its weak cultural uniqueness (unlike Japanese and Chinese Americans)—a heritage of slavery and racism. Furthermore, any student of the racial history of Afro-Americans, Eastern States American Indians, Cubans, Puerto Ricans, and Mexicans, knows that *different* genetic possibilities are not a valid explanation for I.Q. differences.

(10) Jensen, A. *op. cit.* p. 42, "Any observable characteristics, physical or behavioral, is a phenotype, the very existence of which depends upon both genetic and environmental conditions."

(11) Cooper, R. and Zubek, J., "Effects of enriched and restricted early environments on the learning of bright and dull rats" *Canad. J. Psychol.*, 1958, *12*, 159–164.

(12) Ball, W. W. Rouse, *op. cit.*

(13) Herrnstein, Richard. "I.Q., *Atlantic Monthly*, September, 1971.

(14) Jensen, A., *op. cit.* p. 12: "A simple analogy in the physical realm may make (the I.Q.) clear. If we are interested in measuring general athletic ability we can devise a test consisting of running, ball throwing, batting, jumping, weight lifting and so on. We can obtain a score on each one of these and the total for any individual is his 'general athletic ability' score. This score would correspond to the general intelligence score yielded by tests like the Stanford-Binet and the Wechsler scales."

(15) Herrnstein, R., *op. cit.*

(16) Herrnstein, R. *op. cit.*

(17) Herrnstein, R. *op. cit.*

(18) Thorndike, E. L. "Measurement of Twins," *J. Philos. Psychol. Sci. Math.*, 1905, 2, pp. 547–553.

(19) Herrnstein, R., *op. cit.*, Jensen, A., *op. cit.*

(20) Herrnstein, R., *op. cit.*

5

RACIAL DIFFERENCES IN I.Q.: FACT OR ARTIFACT?

BY JANE R. MERCER AND

WAYNE CURTIS BROWN

During the past eight years, we have been involved in an extensive study of mental retardation in the city of Riverside, California, population currently 130,000. We studied the social processes by which a person becomes labeled as a mental retardate by the formal organizations in the community and found about four times more Mexican-Americans and three times more Blacks were being labeled as mentally retarded than would be expected from their percentage in the general population. The rate of labeling for Anglos (English-speaking Caucasians) was only about half the number that would be expected. These disproportions were most pronounced among labeled mental retardates referred to the study by governmental agencies using the statistical model of "normal" and relying heavily on I.Q. tests in making diagnoses, especially in the public schools. Comparable disproportions have been reported for school districts throughout the State of California (California State Department of Education, 1966, 1967, 1968). Ethnic disproportions did not occur among persons referred from privately funded organizations or those relying primarily upon a medical-pathological model of "normal" (Mercer, 1970, 1971a, 1971b, 1971c).

We also found that the Mexican-Americans and Blacks labeled as mentally retarded by community organizations were less subnormal than labeled Anglos. They had a higher average I.Q. test score and fewer physical disabilities than Anglos referred by formal organizations. Persons from minority groups were also more likely than Anglos to have been "diagnosed" as mentally retarded when a low I.Q. test score was the only "symptom" (Mercer, in press, Ch. 11).

In a second portion of our study, we screened a representative sample of 6,907 persons under 50 years of age to determine if they had the clinical "symptoms" of mental retardation—subnormal intelligence and subnormal adaptive behavior. We found that all persons who scored below 70 on the I.Q. test but had passing adaptive behavior (the quasi-retarded) were Mexican-American or Black. Thus, the use of the two-dimensional definition recommended by the American Association for Mental Deficiency significantly reduced ethnic disproportions in rates for clinical retardation.

We also found that I.Q. test scores were correlated .50 with a set of 17 socio-cultural variables when all ethnic groups were combined and were correlated .61 for Mexican-Americans, .52 for Blacks, and .31 for Anglos when analyzed separately. We concluded that I.Q. test scores are significantly influenced by the socio-cultural background of the person being evaluated and that socio-cultural background should be taken into account when interpreting the meaning of a particular person's clinical scores. On the basis of these findings, we have proposed a system of pluralistic assessment in which persons would be classified by their socio-cultural background and their individual I.Q. test scores would then be interpreted in relation to the performance of other persons from comparable socio-cultural backgrounds who presumably have had similar opportunities to acquire the knowledge and skills covered by the typical American "intelligence" test.

Such pluralistic assessment procedures are based on the assumption that the distribution of the genetic potential for learning is essentially identical in all racial and ethnic groups and that the differences now found in the average performance of groups from different ethnic and racial backgrounds are the function of the heavily Anglicized content of typical American I.Q. tests and differential exposure to this content of persons

57

from various American sub-cultures. *Specifically, pluralistic assessment is hypothesizing that (1) differences in "intelligence" test scores among individuals within a particular ethnic-cultural group are the result of the interaction of both genetic and environmental factors but (2) differences between the average I.Q. test scores of different ethnic-cultural groups can be accounted for entirely by environmental factors.* The purpose of this paper is to investigate these two hypotheses.

Before addressing these two hypotheses, it is necessary to clarify three aspects of this issue which are frequently misunderstood and, consequently, confuse discussion: (1) the concepts of genotype and phenotype; (2) the inferential basis for making comparisons and drawing conclusions about the genotypes of different individuals and groups on the basis of their phenotypic performance on an I.Q. test; and (3) the nature and content of American "intelligence" tests.

Clarification of Concepts

Binet and Simon developed the first "intelligence" test in the early 1900's to identify those French children who would not be likely to benefit from regular public school education and should be placed in special schools (Binet and Simon, 1905). Thus, the original purpose for "intelligence" testing was to predict which children would succeed academically. The ability to predict academic achievement through a test score has continued to be the primary criterion for testing the validity of "intelligence" measures. Perhaps the current dialogue about ethnic differences in "intelligence" would have never developed if Binet had labeled his scales general measures of academic readiness rather than measures of "Intelligence." People tend to believe their own labels.

Using the term "intelligence" test to describe a measure of probable academic success has produced serious conceptual confusion. The words "intelligence" and "mental ability" are general terms which, by wide usage, refer to the individual's biological potential for learning, reasoning, understanding, and the like.

Because the connotations associated with the term "intelligence" are more broadly conceived and more complex than academic performance and imply biological differences in mental capacity, brain function, or innate ability, persons have been misled into believing that "intelligence" tests are measures of those inherited factors that constitute the genotype for "intelligence." This semantic confusion was compounded by Goddard, the man who first introduced and promoted the idea of "intelligence" testing in the United States. He interpreted the I.Q. test score as a relatively pure measure of biological potential and such biological interpretations have continued to confuse the testing movement since that time. As a consequence of these semantic confusions, and the history of the testing movement in the United States, an I.Q. test score is frequently, mistakenly, treated as a direct measure of an individual's biological intellectual capacity, his mental ability.

At the present time, biological intellectual capacity cannot be measured directly. Such a measure would require assessment of the genetic component of performance, the genotype. The pure genotype exists only at the moment of conception when the sperm enters the ovum. From that time onward, the genotype is modified by environmental factors. During the intrauterine period, the development of the genetic potential of the organism is influenced by the health and nutrition of the mother and after birth it is influenced by a wide variety of environmental factors. Thus, an individual's genetic potential is always expressed through behavior acquired in a social and cultural setting, his phenotype. A person's performance on an "intelligence" test is phenotypic behavior. His "intelligence" test score is the result of some combination of his genetic intellectual potential and what he has learned through exposure to the kinds of social and cultural experiences which are covered in the questions and performances required in a particular "intelligence" test. On the basis of his phenotypic performance on an "intelligence" test, performance which contains both elements of biological capacity and environmental opportunity, inferences are made about the nature of his genotype, that is, his biological potential.

59

Persons engaged in making clinical diagnoses which go beyond predicting academic achievement are making inferences about the genotypes of persons they are testing on the basis of the performance of the phenotype on an "intelligence" test.

Currently, there is much confusion in the use of the terms "intelligence" and "mental ability" among clinicians, academicians, and lay persons. Some persons use these words to refer to the genotype, that is, biological potential, and others use them to refer to the performance of the phenotype, that is, the I.Q. test score. There are articles in the literature in which the same person uses the words "intelligence" and "mental ability" to refer, simultaneously and interchangeably, to *both* the genotype and the performance of the phenotype, that is, the I.Q. test score. In any discussion of what I.Q. tests measure, it is absolutely essential that the two referents be kept conceptually distinct. It might be best if these two terms were abandoned and were replaced by terms with clearly understood referents. In this article, when referring to the genotype, we will use the term "biological potential." When referring to the performance of the phenotype, we will use the term "I.Q. test score."

The Logical Basis for Making Inferences About Biological Potential from I.Q. Test Scores

Because I.Q. tests cannot measure the genotype directly, clinicians attempt to uncover the nature of the genotype by making inferences about the genotype from the performance of the phenotype. They compare one individual's score on an I.Q. test with the scores of other persons of the same age group and socio-cultural group and try to estimate his biological potential compared to those of other persons. The logic behind these comparisons, in which inferences about genotypes are made from the performance of the phenotypes, is relatively simple. However, the assumptions are rarely, if ever, met in actual practice.

1. If two persons have had equal exposure to opportunities to learn certain types of cognitive, linguistic, and mathematical skills and to acquire certain types of information;

2. If they have value systems which place equal value on the cognitive, linguistic, and mathematical skills being tested, and consequently, are equally motivated to learn these skills and to acquire this information;

3. If they are equally comfortable in and familiar with the demands of the test situation and are equally cooperative, interested, and attentive during the testing;

4. If they are equally free of anxieties, fears, or other emotional disturbances which might interfere with their test performance; and

5. If they are equally free of environmentally produced physical disabilities and organic malfunctions which might interfere with their test performance; then any difference between their performance on a test which measures the extent to which they have learned these cognitive, linguistic and mathematical skills and acquired certain types of knowledge is probably the result of differences in their biological potential, their genotype. Simply stated, if learning opportunities and all other social, cultural, and physical factors are equal, those persons who learn the most and who perform the best on a standard I.Q. test probably have greater biological potential than those who learn least and perform most poorly.

The same assumptions also hold when making comparisons between the average performance of groups of persons. *If* persons in group A and group B have had equal opportunity to acquire the knowledge and skills covered in a standard American I.Q. test; if they equally value that knowledge and those skills and have been equally encouraged and rewarded for learning them; if they are equally motivated to cooperate in a test situation and equally familiar with the demands of the test situation; if they are equally free of emotional disturbances or anxieties which might interfere with their performance; and if they are equally free of environmentally produced physical disabilities which might interfere with their performance; and the average test score of persons in group B is significantly higher than the average score of persons in group A, we might *infer* that group B has greater biological potential than group A. If, however, all things are not equal between group A and B, we cannot infer anything directly from their phenotypic performance, their I.Q. test score, to their genotype. In this situation, we cannot conclude that differences in average I.Q. test scores are necessarily the result of differences in biological potential. Differences could well be due to differences in the environmental factors which were not controlled. This, of course, is the situation when we attempt to determine whether there are genetic differences in intellectual potential between ethnic-cultural groups. Direct inferences from I.Q. test scores to genotype are not valid unless these assumptions are met and all environmental factors extraneous to the genotype are controlled. Even then comparisons should be limited to those performances sampled by a particular test.

One approach to the solution of this dilemma is to try to measure the extent of the inequalities in environmental factors and, if possible, estimate what the average I.Q. test scores would have been *if* all things had been equal. Admittedly, it is difficult to make inferences about genotypes under such circumstances. However, there may be no alternative to such procedures if we are to attempt an explanation of differences between individuals and between groups when all the environmental circumstances for making accurate inferences are not equivalent. This, of course, is our problem in interpreting the meaning of differences in average I.Q. test scores for groups of persons from different ethnic groups in American society. All environmental factors related to performance on a standardized American I.Q. test are not equivalent. Therefore, we are faced with the task of measuring the extent of environmental inequalities and then estimating what the average I.Q. test scores would have been *if* all things had been equal.

The problem of separating genetic from environmental factors in I.Q. test scores has been clearly stated by Jensen.

> Genetic and environmental factors are not properly viewed as being in opposition to each other. Nor are they an "all or none" affair. Any observable characteristic, physical or behavioral, is a

phenotype, the very existence of which depends upon both genetic and environmental conditions. The legitimate question is not whether the characteristic is due to heredity *or* environment, but what proportion of the population variation in the characteristic is attributable to genotypic variation . . . and what proportion is attributable to non-genetic or environmental variation in the population . . . [Jensen, 1969].

Nature and Content of American I.Q. Tests

THE STATISTICAL NORM AND SUB-GROUP DIFFERENCES

(An important aspect of all American I.Q. tests currently in use is that they are based on a statistical model of "normal",) (Mercer, 1972). The statistical model, based on the concept of the normal distribution curve, defines abnormality according to the extent to which an individual varies from the statistical average of a particular group on the characteristic being measured. (To establish the statistical "normal," the investigator specifies the population of persons on whom the norms will be based and then measures a sample of that population. Scores on the measure are organized into a frequency distribution and the average score, that is, the statistical mean, is accepted as the norm) Customarily, persons with scores that differ by not more than one standard deviation above or below the mean are regarded as falling in the "normal range," and comprise approximately 68% of the population. Those whose scores fall more than one, but less than two standard deviations above the mean are classified as "high normals" (approximately 13.6% of the population), and those whose scores fall more than one, but less than two standard deviations below the mean, are labeled as "low normals" (approximately 13.6% of the population). Those whose scores are more than two standard deviations above the mean are "abnormally high" (approximately 2.3% of the population) and those with scores more than two standard deviations below the mean are "abnormally low" (approximately 2.3% of the population). Thus, the characteristics of the particular population on which the test is standardized establish the boundaries of "normal." The norms based on the performance of one population cannot be generalized beyond that population unless the populations are identical on all characteristics significant to the performance being evaluated.

In addition, the statistical model requires that the characteristic being measured be normally distributed. If this is not true, a statistically defined "normal" is misleading. Should the distribution be skewed, the mean will tend to move in the direction of the skew. Even more serious, if the distribution is bimodal or trimodal but is treated as unimodal, distinct distortions will appear. Suppose, for example, we are interested in establishing "normal" weight for the population of the United States but ignore the fact that the distribution is bimodal and that the average female is not as heavy as the average male. Of course, we could calculate a "normal" weight for the combined sexes— but what is its value? The average is too small to tell us much about males and too large to tell us much about females. When a population is split evenly into two different groups, as with sex, bimodality is obvious and not likely to be ignored. However, when sub-groups are small relative to the total population, their impact on the distribution may go unnoticed. In that case, members of sub-groups remain in the combined distribution defined as "abnormal."

Within a multi-ethnic society, the "normal range" established by testing a representative sample of the entire society will reflect the behavior of the most numerous group in the society and, automatically, will categorize the behavior of less numerous groups as "abnormal" if they vary systematically from that of the most numerous group. In American society, the Anglo culture is the culture of the most numerous group. A statistical model will classify the behavior of any sub-group in American society which does not conform to the dominant Anglo cultural norm as "abnormal." The statistical "model" does not take cultural differences into account nor does it allow for cultural pluralism.

When the test designer decides the population on which his test will be standardized or normed, he is explicitly stating the boundaries of the population which he believes will meet the assumptions of the inferential model, that is, the population exposed to similar socio-cultural materials, similar values, and so forth. He is specifying to the test user the socio-cultural group for whom he has designed the test. All of the major American I.Q. tests have been standardized on samples of the Caucasian population of the United States. The standardization group for the Stanford-Binet Intelligence Test "consisted of 3,184 native-born, white subjects." There were approximately 100 subjects at each half-year interval from one and a half to five and a half years, 200 at each age level from 6 through 14, and 100 at each age from 15 through 18. Each age group was equally divided between sexes. Testing was done in 17 communities in 11 states. The final sample which contained no Blacks or Mexican-Americans, was slightly higher in socio-economic level than the census population, and had disproportionately more urban than rural subjects. The 1960 revision did not involve a re-standardization (Terman and Merrill, 1960).

The Wechsler Intelligence Scale for Children (Wechsler, 1949) was standardized on a sample of 2,200 English-speaking Caucasian children. The sample represented all geographic areas of the United States, urban and rural populations, and 9 occupational categories by occupation of the father. No Mexican-American or Black children were included in the standardization sample. The Peabody Picture Vocabulary Test (Dunn, 1965) was standardized on 4,012 white children and youth residing in and around Nashville, Tennessee. The number of children tested at each age level ranged from 92 three-year-olds to 384 eighteen-year-olds. The published norms for the individually administered, Standard-Progressive Matrices are based on a small sample of 735 English children, presumably all Caucasians (Raven, 1960).

By omitting Black and Mexican-American children from the standardization samples of these tests, the test designers have implicitly set those children outside the ethnic and socio-cultural boundaries of the population which they believe fulfill the assumptions of the inferential model. In spite of this fact, psychometrists in public schools and clinics have almost universally used these tests for Black and Mexican-American children as well as for Anglo children and have drawn conclusions about these children's biological potential from their I.Q. test scores without taking socio-cultural differences into account. Academicians have developed theories about biological differences in "intelligence" between ethnic groups on the basis of such tests (Jensen, 1969, Eysenck, 1971). This paper will examine the validity of such direct cross-cultural comparisons.

THE ANGLOCENTRIC CONTENT OF AMERICAN I.Q. TESTS

Having defined his target population, the test designer has specified the cultural milieu from which he will select items for his test. Binet selected questions for his test which would cover a wide variety of skills and information which he presumed most French children would have had an opportunity to acquire. Binet's original test was not appropriate for use in an Anglo culture. Therefore, Terman not only translated the test into English, but made other modifications in Binet's test before it was usable in the United States. Just as Binet had French culture in mind when he constructed his original test, so, implicitly, subsequent test makers have attempted to include a wide variety of behaviors valued in the cultural heritage of the group for whom their tests were being designed and to include behaviors which most persons in that socio-cultural group would have had an opportunity to learn.

American I.Q. tests have, inevitably, included items and procedures which reflect the abilities and skills valued by the American core culture. This "core culture" consists mainly of the cultural patterns of that segment of the population consisting of white, Anglo-Saxon Protestants whose social status today has become middle and upper middle class. This cultural domination dates back to colonial times and has never been seriously threatened (Gordon, 1964). This is the group on which the tests were standardized.

What kinds of abilities and skills does the "core culture" value?

66

Of the 128 intelligence tests listed in Buros, 58 were measures of general intelligence with no subtests. Measures of general intelligence are all highly loaded with verbal skills in the English language and knowledge about the Anglo culture. Of the 70 tests that have subtests, 77% have subtests entitled Vocabulary, Language, or Verbal. Fifty-one percent have subtests entitled Arithmetic, Quantitative, or Numerical and 53% have subtests entitled Reasoning, Logic, of Conceptual Thinking (Buros, 1965). The number of subtests measuring skills such as manual dexterity or mechanical ability is negligible. To rate as "intelligent" in American society one must be highly verbal in English language, and adept at mathematical manipulations. In the American "core culture" speed of performance is perceived as a sign of brightness. Performance on many tasks on American I.Q. tests are rated by how fast the person completes them. One receives little official credit for musical, artistic, or mechanical abilities. The ability to live amicably with other human beings counts not at all in the psychometric test situation. The Anglocentrism inherent in the American mental tests most frequently used for diagnosing "intelligence" has been thoroughly documented (Altus, 1949; Darcy, 1963; Eells, 1951).

The Wechsler Intelligence Scale for Children which was used in the present study, was copyrighted in 1949 and is currently one of the two most widely used individually administered tests for evaluating American children. It consists of 12 subtests, 11 of which were used in the current study. The test yields a Full Scale I.Q. which includes scores on all subtests; a Verbal I.Q. which includes scores on 6 of the subtests; and a Performance I.Q. which includes scores on 5 of the subtests. The content of each of the subtests will be briefly described to illustrate the Anglocentric nature of the test and to provide a background for understanding the data analysis in the later portions of this paper. The first six subtests are those included in the calculation of the Verbal I.Q. and all of these subtests, except Digit Span, are heavily loaded with academic materials.

The Information Subtest consists of 30 questions which require a sufficiently large English vocabulary to understand such words as rubies, COD, barometer, average, hieroglyphic, lien, and turpentine. Information is asked about two American holidays (the 4th of July and the date of Labor Day), English literature (Romeo and Juliet), English weights and measures (a dozen and a ton), United States and world geography, and miscellaneous information about world history and biology.

The Comprehension Subtest measures the extent to which a child has internalized certain American values. The test consists of a series of 14 hypothetical situations in which the child is to tell "why" certain behaviors are better than others or to describe what a person "should" do in various situations. The "correct" responses are those that reflect a value system which holds that big children should not fight with smaller children; brick houses are better than wooden houses; criminals are dangerous and should be punished; the lives of women and children are more important than the lives of men in a shipwreck; paying by check is better than paying by cash; giving to an organized charity is better than helping individuals; giving a person a job because he makes a high score on a test is better than giving him a job because he is your friend or a member of your family; a democratic government is better than other types of governments because you get better qualified persons through election; and that promises should be kept to preserve the contractual nature of relationships between individuals. These questions presuppose not only a knowledge of the value system of the Anglo core culture but agreement with that value system.

The Arithmetic Subtest consists of a series of 16, increasingly difficult, timed questions which require that a child be able to add, subtract, multiply, and divide rapidly in his head after he comprehends the nature of the arithmetical manipulation required by a question which is asked in English. Questions require that a child know the numerical equivalents for English terms such as half, one-third, two-thirds, quarter, and dozen.

The Similarities Subtest consists of 12 pairs of nouns. The child is asked to explain how the objects symbolized by those nouns are alike. It is assumed he is familiar with the English words and the objects to which they refer. The relationship between the pairs of nouns becomes increasingly attenuated. Responses are scored by their degree of generalization. A child socialized in an environment in which most conversations deal with concrete situations and day-to-day necessities will have had little experience in discussing abstract relationships between various categories of objects.

The Vocabulary Subtest consists of 40 English words, mostly nouns, which the child is asked to define. The opportunity to learn about the actual objects symbolized by these nouns is not equally present in all segments of society—fur, diamond, umbrella, donkey, sword, nitroglycerin, microscope, and so forth. Many of the words on the list would be encountered only in a written context and are not likely to be used conversationally—shilling, belfry, hara-kiri, ballast, catacomb, mantis, vesper, chattel, and so forth.

The Digit Span Subtest asks the child to recall a series of numbers and repeat them after the examiner. The initial series contains 3 digits, increasing to 9 digits. The child is then asked to repeat the digits backwards. The backwards series runs from 2 digits to 8 digits.

The Performance I.Q. is based on the following five subtests. They do not require the use of English, except in understanding the instructions. To this extent, they are less Anglocentric than most of the verbal subtests which assume a high level of familiarity with the English language. However, the Performance Subtests are all timed.

Picture Completion consists of a series of 20 line drawings of objects which have some part missing. Some objects are relatively familiar—a hand, a human face, a coat, a door, and a cat. Others are less familiar—a fish, a rooster, a thermometer, an umbrella, and a cow. The child is given 15 seconds to either name or point to the missing part.

Picture Arrangement consists of sets of cards, which, when arranged in the proper order, either make a complete picture of an object, or, in the more difficult items, tell a story. There is a time limit and the child receives a fixed series of bonuses for faster performances. A child who has read American comic books and seen movie cartoons would have an advantage on this task.

The Block Design Subtest expects the child to arrange colored blocks so that they duplicate various designs formed by blocks arranged by the examiner. The easiest design involves arranging 4 blocks. The more difficult designs involve arranging 9 blocks and replicating a design pictured in two dimensions on a card. All performances have an upper time limit and bonuses are given for faster completions.

Object Assembly consists of 4 puzzles increasing in difficulty from 5 to 7 pieces. Objects depicted are a man, a horse, a human face, and a car—all familiar to most American children regardless of cultural heritage. Again, performance is timed.

Coding asks a child to fill in or to substitute one set of symbols for another set of symbols. For example, two lines are to be filled in for each ball, one line filled in for each star, and so forth. Children are scored according to the number of correct insertions or substitutions they can make within a given time period.

The two other I.Q. tests used in the present study were Raven's Standard Progressive Matrices and the Peabody Picture Vocabulary Test. The Progressive Matrices, developed in England, is completely non-verbal except for explaining the relatively simple instructions. A child is shown a series of patterns, each with a blank space in the middle. He is asked to point to one of four designs which will fit in and correctly complete the blank area in the larger design. Designs become increasingly complex. There are no time limits. The child's score is the number of correct responses. The test can be administered in any language by simply translating the simple instructions into the appropriate language and it does not have a specifically Anglocentric content. However, the questions cover only a narrow range of behaviors.

70

The Peabody Picture Vocabulary Test is a test of English vocabulary which requires that the child point to the one of 4 pictures which depicts the meaning of a word spoken by the examiner. There are 150 words on the list standardized for ages 3 years 3 months through 17 years 6 months. The range appropriate for children in our sample was approximately from words 20 through 80 on the list. About 80% of the words are nouns, and the remainder are the present participle form of various verbs and some adjectives and adverbs.

This test is more culturally complex than the vocabulary subtest of the WISC. The child must be familiar with a wide variety of objects, for example, ambulance, tweezers, wasp, captain, hive, reel, idol, casserole, scholar, and observatory. He must also be able to decode the pictures to determine which one best represents such words as filing, harvesting, soldering, assistance, dissatisfaction, astonishment, and horror. In some cases, the words in the vocabulary list are not the words most commonly used in spoken English for the objects which are pictured, for example, shears, chef, cobbler, and hydrant. In the case of some adjectives, the picture is of an object which the adjective frequently modifies. For example, the correct response to the word "thoroughbred" is the picture of a horse.

This brief review of the content of the I.Q. tests used in the present study is sufficient to demonstrate the extent to which "intelligence" as operationalized in these tests means familiarity with the subtleties of the English language, knowledge of the Anglo culture, and acceptance of the Anglo value system. Six of the eleven Wechsler Intelligence Scale for Children subtests assume that the child will respond competitively to the Anglo value which holds that all tasks should be completed as rapidly as possible and that the smartest person is the one who does things the fastest. A child who has not internalized this Anglo value, and does not place much importance on seeing how quickly he can put a puzzle or a block design together would rate as "unintelligent" on these measures. Some of the subtests are more Anglicized than others. The Vocabulary, Information, and Similarities Subtests of the Weschler Intelligence Scale for Children and the Peabody Picture Vocabulary Test have the greatest English language and Anglo culture content.

Samples and I.Q. Measures Used for the Present Analysis

The data for the analysis was collected between February, 1966 and June, 1967 as part of two separate studies, neither of which were concerned in any way with the issues addressed in this paper. During the school year 1966–67, 598 Mexican-American, 339 Black, and 576 Anglo elementary school children in the Riverside Unified School District, Riverside, California, were tested as part of a study of school desegregation being conducted by the senior author (Professor J. R. Mercer). The Anglo children were randomly selected from 11 predominantly Anglo elementary schools in the district which had been designated as "receiving" schools in the desegregation plan. The Mexican-American and Black children included all the children attending the three segregated minority elementary schools which then existed in the district and a sample of Mexican-American and Black children already enrolled in the predominantly Anglo "receiving" schools because they lived in ethnically integrated neighborhoods.

An attempt was made to interview, individually, both parents of each child to secure information about the family and about the child. In addition, each child was interviewed, individually, in two one-hour sessions. During these sessions the Peabody Picture Vocabulary Test and Raven's Standard Progressive Matrices were administered.

A team of psychometrists tested each child in the desegregation sample using the Wechsler Intelligence Scale for Children under a separate contract with the United States Public Health Service for the purpose of estimating the validity of certain psychological measures given in the health examination survey of children 6–11 years of age. The fact that the data for the

72

two studies was collected on the same children proved to be a fortuitous circumstance making the present analysis possible. All psychometrists had completed regular university courses in test administration and were also given supplementary training by a psychological consultant from the Public Health Service to assure that testing and scoring procedures would be standardized. All psychometrists were Anglo and all tests were given in English. Consequently, the test situation paralleled the usual test situation found in the public schools.

A subset of 540 children, 180 from each of the three ethnic groups, was randomly selected from among the children in the larger sample for the present analysis. This subset was selected so that there would be an equal number of children from each ethnic group, only one child from each nuclear family, and only children for whom we had complete information from parent and child interviews.

According to Table 1, the phenotypic performance, that is, I.Q. test scores, of the Mexican-American and Black children tested in Riverside was significantly lower on all the measures than the phenotypic performance of the Anglo children. The mean Full Scale WISC I.Q. for the Anglo sample was 107.5 compared to 91.3 for Mexican-American children and 91.9 for Black children. The Anglo children in Riverside come mainly from middle and upper middle status homes. Their fathers are mainly white collar and professional workers and have more than a high school education.

Ethnic differences were greatest on those subtests of the WISC with the heaviest "Anglo" content—Information, Similarities, and Vocabulary. Black children generally did slightly better than Mexican-American children on the Verbal tests while Mexican-American children did slightly better than Black children on the timed Performance tests. Both did less well than Anglo children. Differences on the Peabody Picture Vocabulary Test were even greater than on the WISC. Anglo children had a mean of 117.3, Mexican-American children a mean of 82.7, and Black children a mean of 93.0. Apparently, Tennessee norms are not very appropriate for California Anglo children and the content

TABLE 1 *Mean Scores of the Children in the Three Ethnic Groups on the I.Q. Tests and Subtests Used as Dependent Variables*

	Mexican-American (N = 180)		Black (N = 180)		Anglo (N = 180)		Reliability Coefficient Used In Analysis[a]
	Mean	Standard Deviation	Mean	Standard Deviation	Mean	Standard Deviation	
WISC							
Full Scale I.Q.	91.3	13.5	91.9	12.3	107.5	11.9	.94
Verbal I.Q.	88.2	13.8	90.4	13.0	105.5	12.1	.99
Performance I.Q.	96.3	13.9	92.8	12.7	108.3	12.8	.88
Verbal Subtests							
Information	7.8	2.9	8.6	2.6	10.7	2.8	.76
Comprehsnsion	8.0	3.1	8.7	2.8	9.9	3.1	.68
Arithmetic	9.0	2.9	8.9	2.9	11.0	2.6	.75
Similarities	8.5	3.2	9.3	2.7	11.7	3.1	.75
Vocabulary	7.4	3.0	8.8	2.9	11.8	3.0	.86
Digit Span	7.8	2.6	8.6	3.1	11.0	2.8	.56
Performance Subtests							
Picture Completion	8.8	3.0	8.4	2.7	10.6	3.2	.64
Picture Arrangement	9.5	3.0	9.2	2.8	11.2	2.8	.72
Block Design	9.3	3.0	8.5	2.8	11.5	2.8	.86
Object Assembly	9.7	2.7	8.9	2.8	11.2	2.7	.66
Coding	10.1	3.1	9.8	2.8	11.5	3.0	.60
Raven's Progressive Matrices	50.9	11.0	49.5	9.8	58.9	9.9	.88
Peabody Picture Vocabulary	82.7	20.3	93.0	18.5	117.3	18.6	.75

[a] Reliability Coefficients for the WISC are the average reliabilities reported for ages 7½, 10½, and 13½ (Wechsler, 1949, p. 13); for the Peabody are the average reliability for ages 5 through 13 (Dunn, 1965, p. 30); for the Raven's the reliability for 13 year olds (Raven, 1960, p. 16).

is especially culture-bound for Mexican-American children. Similar ethnic differences appeared for the Raven's Standard Progressive Matrices but were less marked. All differences between Anglo children and Mexican-American and Black children were greater than would be expected by chance ($p < .01$).

The reliability coefficients used in the analysis for correction for attentuation of correlation coefficients due to the unreliability of measures are given in the right hand column of Table 1. For the WISC, the reliability coefficients are the average reliability reported for ages $7\frac{1}{2}$, $10\frac{1}{2}$, and $13\frac{1}{2}$ (Wechsler, 1949, p. 13). The reliability coefficients for the Peabody are the average reliability for ages 5 through 13 (Dunn, 1965, p. 30). The reliability for the Raven's is that for 13 year olds (Raven, 1960, p. 16).

Measures of Environmental Variables

Earlier in this paper, we postulated that at least five types of conditions must be held constant before inferences can be made about one group's biological potential by comparing its phenotypic performance, that is, mean I.Q. test score with that of other groups. Such comparisons can be made only if there is (1) equal exposure to opportunities to learn the culture-bound materials in the test, (2) equal participation in the values and motivational systems assumed by the test, (3) equal freedom from anxiety and emotional disturbance, (4) equal familiarity with and comfort in the test situation, and (5) equal freedom from environmentally produced physical disabilities that might interfere with performance. To the extent that any group's performance is depressed by the presence of these factors, valid inferences about genotypic potential are not possible.

From the parent and child interviews, we secured information which we organized into 9 measures. Six were measures of the child's exposure to Anglo cultural material, two were measures of his exposure to Anglo values, and one was a measure of his anxiety level. Although the items included in 4 of these measures were originally identified through factor analysis, we

75

did not use factor scores in the present analysis because factor scores are difficult to replicate in another study.[1]

The chief disadvantage of using summated rather than factor scores is that the former are more highly intercorrelated than the latter. Consequently, we will not be able to estimate the independent contribution of each individual environmental variable to any specific solution. However, being able to make such estimates is not critical to the present discussion.

The reliability of each indicator was computed by the split-half technique and corrections for the full length of the measure were made using the Spearman-Brown formula (Guilford, 1965, p. 458). All correlations presented in subsequent analyses have been corrected for attentuation resulting from the unreliability of measures and the reader should supply the qualifying phrase "corrected for attentuation" whenever correlations are reported in the text.

INDICATORS OF CHILD'S EXPOSURE TO ANGLO CULTURAL MATERIALS

Mother's Participation in Formal Organizations. We assumed that each elementary school child's acquaintance with the Anglo core-culture would be mediated primarily through his mother. We reasoned that the extent of the mother's exposure to and participation in the formal organizations of Anglo society would serve as one indirect indicator of the extent to which her child had been exposed to the cultural materials of Anglo society.

[1] An earlier analysis of the data was reported at a Seminar at the Brookhaven National Laboratory presented for the Annual Conference of The Council for the Advancement of Science Writing, November 18, 1971. The earlier analysis utilized 5 factor scores based on a factor analysis of 28 measures of emotional, sociocultural, and test situation variables and two additional variables—family size and living in a minority segregated neighborhood. Four of the factor scores used in that analysis are parallel to four variables used in the present report: Mother's Formal Participation, Cultural Barriers, Individualistic Achievement Values, and Anxiety. A fifth factor used in the earlier report, Test-Wise Behavior, was not used in the present analysis because critics of that earlier paper argued that ratings given by a psychologist at the time of the testing would, inevitably, be influenced in unknown ways by the psychologist's knowledge of how well the child had done on the test.

We did not include measures of participation in informal social groups such as neighborhood and kinship groups. Such interactions would not necessarily lead to familiarity with Anglo society for members of minority groups living in segregated neighborhoods.

This indicator consists of five measures of the mother's formal participation in the Anglo community: the total number of child-oriented groups, such as PTA, Scouts, and study clubs; the total number of church affiliated groups; the total number of ethnically mixed social groups; the mother's weighted participation score, (which gives higher weight to participation in those organizations in which she holds an office or serves on a committee); and the mother's participation as a citizen as measured by her being registered and voting in local, state, and national elections. This indicator had a reliability of .61. Corrected for attenuation, the mother's formal participation was correlated .28 with the Full Scale WISC I.Q. for Mexican-American children, .21 for Black children, and .12 for Anglo children.

Minority Neighborhood. Another more direct indicator of exposure to Anglo culture was provided by the neighborhood in which the child was living. We reasoned that a minority child who lives in an integrated neighborhood containing some Anglo families will have greater exposure to Anglo cultural materials and values than a child who lives in a segregated, minority neighborhood and attends a segregated, minority school. This second indicator of exposure to Anglo culture was scored as a simple dichotomy. Children who lived in neighborhoods which had 60% or more minority population were scored as living in a segregated minority neighborhood. Those living in all other neighborhoods were scored as living in a majority neighborhood (United States Census, 1960). Neighborhood of residence was correlated .14 with Full Scale WISC I.Q. for Mexican-American children, .25 for Black children, and .07 for Anglo children.

Cultural Barriers. We also reasoned that a child who lives with a mother who speaks English fluently and is more informed about the public schools which her child attends will also be more exposed to the cultural materials of the dominant culture

77

than a child from a family which seldom or never speaks English, and knows little about the Anglo public schools. This scale is most highly correlated with the phenotypic performance of Mexican-American children. The scale had a reliability of .53. It correlated —.28 with Full Scale WISC I.Q. for Mexican-American children, and —.25 for Black children. There was no correlation for Anglo children because there were few cultural barriers for any of them.

Socio-economic Status. The most significant link between any family and the larger society is the occupational status of the head-of-household and the education of the head-of-household. The higher the occupational status of the head, the more knowledgeable he will be about the social structure of American society, the role behaviors rewarded in American society, and the information and skills needed to succeed in the mainstream of American life. The greater the amount of formal education which he has had in American schools, the more familiar he will be with the cultural materials of Anglo society and the more he will be able to convey his knowledge to his children. Occupation of the head was rated using the Duncan Socio-economic Index (Reiss, 1961) and education was rated by the total number of years of formal education. The reliability of our measure of socio-economic status was .79. It was correlated .26 with Full Scale WISC I.Q. for Mexican-American children, .22 for Black children, and .21 for Anglo children.

Urbanization measures the extent to which a child's parents were exposed to American urban society during their childhood. Two types of information were included in this index: whether the parents were reared in northern or western United States vs southern United States or Mexico and whether they were reared in a rural or an urban setting. The reliability of this indicator was relatively low, .32. It was not correlated with Full Scale WISC I.Q. for Mexican-American or Anglo children, but was correlated .12 for Black children.

Home Ownership was another measure that proved significant. It correlated .18 with Full Scale WISC I.Q. for Mexican-American children, .16 for Black children, and .17 for Anglo children.

Exposure to Anglo Values. We had two indicators of the child's exposure to Anglo cultural values—a measure of his mother's values, and a measure of family structure.

Individualistic Achievement Values. This variable consists of questions selected from a variety of measures of values (Turner 1964; Strodtbeck, 1958; Srole, 1952; Lenski, 1961). Mothers who had internalized Anglo values expressed the following attitudes: They believed problems can be actively mastered and rejected the notion that there is little use in planning because success is a matter of fate. They did not feel powerless to influence the course of events and were not anomic or pessimistic about the future. They believed it was more important for their sons to have a job with a good chance for advancement and achievement and were less concerned about job security or large incomes. They also felt that grown children should not remain close to their parents and should not value their relationship with their parents more than job opportunities or loyalty to a marital partner. The pattern of correlations was quite consistent. Mothers from minority groups who had value orientations consistent with those of the Anglo core-culture were more likely to have children who performed well on American I.Q. tests. This measure had a reliability of .70 and correlated .25 with Full Scale WISC I.Q. for Mexican-American children, .19 for Black children, and .14 for Anglo children.

Family Structure. This variable was scored as a dichotomy; biological parents and children vs all other types of family structure. This measure correlated .12 with Full Scale WISC I.Q. for Mexican-American children, .14 for Black children, and .12 for Anglo children.

Anxiety. The child's anxiety level was measured during an interview with the child conducted one year prior to the I.Q. testing. Questions were selected from items in the scales developed by Sarason to measure anxiety in elementary school children (Sarason, 1969). The 15 questions in the school anxiety scale asked about fears associated with school; fear of reciting; fear of making mistakes; fear of taking tests; fear of not being promoted; and so forth. The 15 questions in the general anxiety scale inquired about a variety of fears: fear of being left alone; fear of animals; fear of sickness and accidents; fear of the dark; fear of loss of parents; and so forth.

Anxiety, whatever its source, tends to depress test performance and to make it difficult to assess what a child's performance would have been under optimal conditions. Probably no single variable has been given more consideration in the psychometric literature. Wechsler devotes an entire chapter to discussing problems in the differential diagnosis of mentally ill or disturbed persons (Wechsler, 1958, p. 155–198). In our study, the measure of anxiety had a reliability of .78 and correlated —.20 with Full Scale WISC I.Q. for Mexican-American children, —.27 for Black children, and —.23 for Anglo children.

Two variables in the inferential model which we did not include in the present analysis were physical disability and test-wise behavior. Mothers were asked a series of questions about each child's illnesses, operations, and accidents and questions about his vision, hearing, ambulation, seizures, and arm-hand use in self care. Although scores on this physical disabilities scale were correlated with Full Scale WISC I.Q. for the entire sample, there were no differences across ethnic group and it added nothing to the analysis.

Table 2 shows that the Anglo children in our sample were in a significantly more favored position on all the environmental variables than Mexican-American and Black children. On six of the environmental, that is, socio-cultural variables, the mean for the Black sample falls between the Anglo mean and the Mexican-American mean. Anglo children have much greater exposure to Anglo cultural materials as measured by their mother's participation in formal organizations with Black mothers in the middle and Mexican-American mothers lowest. (Mean Anglo scores 192.8 compared to 155.9 for Black and 126.1 for Mexican-American children). Anglo children suffer few cultural barriers (Anglo mean score 2.3 compared to 3.2 for Blacks and 4.0 for Mexican-Americans) and are more exposed to individualistic achievement values (Mean 65.3 for Anglo mothers compared to 58.3 for Black mothers and 53.0 for Mexican-American

TABLE 2 Mean Scores for the Children in the Three Ethnic Groups and Correlations with Full Scale WISC I.Q. Within Ethnic Group for the Nine Environmental Variables[a]

Environmental Variables	Mexican-American			Black			Anglo			Reliability Coefficient
	Mean	Standard Deviation	r with Full Scale I.Q.	Mean	Standard Deviation	r with Full Scale I.Q.	Mean	Standard Deviation	r with Full Scale I.Q.	
Mother's Formal Participation	126.1	89.1	.28	155.9	99.2	.21	192.8	78.3	.12	.61
Individualistic Achievement Values	53.0	8.1	.25	58.3	8.5	.19	65.3	4.9	.14	.70
Segregated Neighborhood	.1	.3	.14	.3	.5	.25	.9	.2	.07	
Socio-economic Status	49.9	24.2	.26	76.8	28.6	.22	120.3	33.6	.21	.79
Cultural Barriers	4.0	2.1	−.28	3.2	1.3	−.25	2.3	.6	.00	.53
Anxiety	13.4	5.9	−.29	12.7	6.0	−.27	10.3	5.9	−.23	.78
Home Ownership	.7	.5	.18	.5	.5	.16	.9	.3	.17	
Urbanization	1.6	.7	−.01	1.3	.7	−.03	1.5	.6	.12	.32
Family Structure	2.6	.9	.12	2.1	1.3	.14	2.7	.8	.12	.87

[a] All correlations corrected for attenuation due to the unreliability of measures.

mothers). Socio-economic differences are very large. The Anglo mean is 120.3 compared to 76.8 for Black and 49.9 for Mexican-American heads-of-household. The mean score for segregated minority neighborhood is .1 for Mexican-American, .3 for Black, and .9 for Anglo children. Both Black and Mexican-American children are significantly more fearful and anxious in public school situations than Anglo children. The mean anxiety score was 13.4 for Mexican-American children, 12.7 for Black children, and 10.3 for Anglo children.

On three environmental variables, the mean for the Black sample was below the Mexican-American mean. The parents of Black children are least urbanized (Black mean 1.3; Anglo mean 1.5; and Mexican-American mean 1.6). A smaller proportion of Black families own their homes (Black mean .5; Mexican-American mean .7; and Anglo mean .9) and Black children come from more irregular family structures (Black mean 2.1; Mexican-American mean 2.6; and Anglo mean 2.7). These three socio-cultural variables were used only in those analyses containing Black children and not in analyses containing Mexican-American children. When standard scores were used for all environmental measures, results were similar to those secured with the raw scores.

The Influence of Environmental Factors on I.Q. Test Scores Within Ethnic Group

There are two separate questions to be answered in relation to the influence of environmental factors on I.Q. test performance. The first question is to determine the percentage of the variance in the I.Q. test scores of persons of the same racial and cultural group which can be accounted for by environmental factors. This question concerns *within-ethnic-group variation* and asks whether we can make valid comparisons between the I.Q. test scores of children from the same ethnic group for the purpose of making inferences about probable differences in their biological potential.

The second question is to determine whether the differences between the average I.Q. test scores of different racial and cultural groups can be explained by differences in the environmental factors impinging on these groups. When the environmental factors have been controlled, do differences in the mean I.Q. test scores persist? This question concerns *between-ethnic-group differences* and asks whether we can make valid comparisons between the average I.Q. test scores of persons from different ethnic groups for the purpose of making inferences about probable differences in their biological potential. This section will discuss *within-ethnic-group differences*. The next section will discuss *between-ethnic-group differences*. ⏎

When we talk about *within-ethnic-group differences,* we are asking, for example, what factors account for one Black child having an I.Q. test score of 110, another Black child having an I.Q. test score of 90, another Black child having an I.Q. test score of 103, and so forth. To answer this question, we attempt to determine, statistically, how much of all the differences between the I.Q. test scores, that is, the phenotypes, of the 180 individual children within each ethnic group are correlated with the environmental, that is, socio-cultural variables, we have measured and how much of the total difference cannot be accounted for by these variables. Correlational analysis is the usual statistical method for answering this type of question. The square of a correlation coefficient indicates the percentage of the differences among the scores of individuals which can be accounted for by whatever independent variables are used in the analysis.

We do not expect that the size of the correlations will be exactly identical for each ethnic group because the size of a correlation coefficient varies with the heterogeneity of the sample being measured. The percentage of variance accounted for by environmental factors will tend to be larger in those groups which are environmentally heterogeneous than in those groups which are homogeneous. This principle is easy to understand if we imagine a hypothetical group of children reared under identical conditions. Suppose that, from the time of conception, a group of children receive equivalent physical and medical care, are similarly loved and protected at home and at school so that they have low levels of school anxiety and are equally

83

comfortable in a test situation, and also receive identical socialization in language, arithmetic, history, and so forth. Because their environments have been identical, this hypothetical situation would meet the assumptions of the inferential model for making estimates of genotypes from phenotypes. The correlation between each of the measures of environmental factors and I.Q. test score would be zero because the environmental measures would be the same for every child. Any differences among their I.Q. test scores would be related to differences in their biological capacity for learning. Of course, such a situation never actually occurs, even for children reared in the same family. Herrnstein presents a clear discussion of this issue (Herrnstein, 1971).

SUMMARY OF FINDINGS FROM "HERITABILITY" STUDIES OF WITHIN-GROUP VARIANCE

The most common approach to estimating the percentage of the within-group variance in I.Q. test scores which can be accounted for by environmental factors has been to study the correlations between the I.Q. test scores of persons who have varying degrees of biological relationship to each other. Such heritability studies provide an estimate of the amount of variance in I.Q. test scores which can be accounted for by genetic factors and the residual or unexplained variance is presumed to be due to differences in environmental conditions.

Jensen reported the findings from 141 heritability studies and reached the conclusion that approximately 80% of the within-group variance in I.Q. test scores of the Caucasian populations examined in those studies was related to genetic factors. His conclusion rests primarily on his review of studies of monozygotic twins. Since monozygotic twins have exactly the same genes, any differences between their I.Q. test scores must be due to nongenetic factors. Basing his judgement on four studies of monozygotic twins reared apart, he concluded that "Seventy-five percent of the variance can be said to be due to genetic variations (heritability) and 25% to environmental variations" (Jensen, 1969, p. 50). He then looked at the correlation of I.Q. test scores of unrelated

84

children who were reared together and concluded, "The proportion of I.Q. variance due to environment is .24; and the remainder, $1.00 - .24 = .76$ is due to heredity" (Jensen, 1969, p. 51). When he applied his heritability formula to all of the correlations of monozygotic and dizygotic twins reported in the literature, he found "an average heritability of .80 for intelligence test scores" (Jensen, 1969, p. 51).

All of these studies were conducted on Caucasian samples using persons from similar socio-cultural environments. None of these studies were done on Mexican-American or Black populations. The Caucasian samples approximated the inferential model for comparing phenotypes to estimate differences in genotypes. For example, the Burt Study, which had the largest sample of monozygotic twins separated at birth, consisted of English children, reared in England, attending English schools, and sharing a common language and culture. Their environments differed only by social class within a single racial and cultural group (Burt, 1966). Because similar "heritability" studies have not been done on Black and Mexican-American samples, we do not know if similar "heritability" coefficients would occur in these ethnic groups. There is no data.

FINDINGS FOR THE RIVERSIDE SAMPLES

We have used a different approach from that used in the heritability studies. We have investigated the extent to which individuals within each of the three ethnic groups meet the assumptions of the inferential model. We have estimated the percentage of the variance in the I.Q. test scores of children within each ethnic group which can be accounted for by differences in their exposure to Anglo society and Anglo values and to their anxiety levels.

Table 3 presents the multiple correlation coefficients predicting WISC I.Q.'s and subtest scores, Peabody I.Q.'s and scores on the Raven's from the nine environmental variables described earlier. These multiple correlation coefficients range from .18 to .66.

Table 3 reports the number of environmental variables which

85

TABLE 3 *Stepwise Multiple Correlation Coefficients Using I.Q. Test Scores as Dependent Variables and Environmental Measures as Independent Variables*[a]

	Mexican-American (N = 180)			Black (N = 180)			Anglo (N = 180)		
	# Significant Variables	R	% Variance	# Significant Variables	R	% Variance	# Significant Variables	R	% Variance
WISC									
Full Scale I.Q.	6	.48	22.6	9	.44	19.6	6	.37	13.6
Verbal I.Q.	6	.51	25.9	9	.43	18.9	6	.42	17.3
Performance I.Q.	6	.35	12.1	8	.39	15.2	6	.25	6.0
Subtest Scaled Scores									
Information	6	.62	38.4	9	.55	30.1	6	.49	24.2
Comprehension	6	.43	18.2	9	.43	18.8	6	.35	12.6
Arithmetic	6	.43	18.8	9	.44	19.1	5	.22	4.8
Similarities	6	.48	23.2	8	.46	21.3	6	.43	18.7
Vocabulary	6	.55	30.5	9	.46	21.2	6	.40	16.0
Digit Span	6	.33	10.8	8	.43	18.1	6	.25	6.3
Picture Completion	6	.56	31.5	9	.36	13.2	5	.31	9.4
Picture Arrangement	6	.24	5.7	9	.61	37.0	6	.29	8.6
Block Design	6	.47	21.7	9	.52	26.7	5	.18	3.4
Object Assembly	5	.30	9.0	9	.50	25.0	6	.21	4.3
Coding	6	.24	5.6	9	.42	17.6	6	.27	7.3
Peabody Picture Vocabulary	6	.66	44.1	8	.49	24.3	6	.45	20.0
Raven's Progressive Matrices	5	.38	14.3	9	.39	15.5	6	.22	4.8

[a] All correlations corrected for attenuation due to unreliability of measures (Guilford, 1965).

make a statistically significant contribution to the multiple correlation coefficient. Environmental variables account for 22.6% of the variance in Full Scale WISC I.Q.'s for Mexican-American children; 25.9% of the variance in Verbal I.Q.'s; 12.1% of the variance in Performance I.Q.'s; 44.1% of the variance in Peabody I.Q.'s; and 14.3% of the variance on the Raven's. It required six variables to reach the maximum multiple correlation coefficient for most tests.

Environmental variables account for 19.6% of the variance in the Full Scale WISC I.Q.'s of Black children; 18.9% of the variance in the Verbal I.Q.'s; 15.2% of the variance in the Performance I.Q.'s; 24.3% of the variance in the Peabody I.Q.'s; and 15.5% of the variance in Raven's I.Q.'s. In most cases, all nine environmental variables made a significant contribution.

For Anglo children, most of the within-group variance is accounted for by 6 environmental variables. Socio-cultural factors account for 13.6% of the variance in Full Scale WISC I.Q.'s; 17.3% of the variance in Verbal I.Q.'s; 6.0% of the variance in Performance I.Q.'s; 20.0% of the variance in Peabody I.Q.'s; and 4.8% of the variance in Raven's scores. The reason for these lower correlations is clarified in Table 2. Anglo children were more similar to each other on several of the socio-cultural variables than were Black and Mexican-American children. This cultural homogeneity reduces the size of the correlation, and indicates that the environments of Anglo children more nearly meet the assumptions of the inferential model than do the backgrounds of Mexican-American and Black children.

The overall percentages for estimated environmental contribution to variance in I.Q. test scores from the Riverside data are approximately the same as estimates for environmental factors made by Jensen in his review of "heritability" studies done only on socio-culturally homogeneous Anglo samples.

As shown in Figure 1, Jensen estimated 20% to 30% of the within-ethnic-group variance was the result of environmental factors. Estimates from the multiple correlations done from the Riverside study vary from 14% to 23%. The unexplained variance, which includes genetic factors, ranges from 77% to 86% in the

FIGURE 1 *Chart Depicting Findings from Two Approaches to the Study of Within-Ethnic-Group Differences*

Estimates from the Heritability Studies[a]

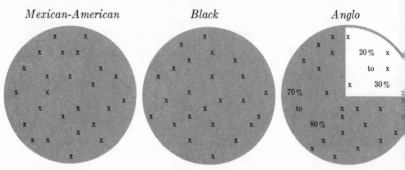

Mexican-American	Black	Anglo
No data on Heritability	No data on Heritability	70%–80% Heritabilit 20%–30% Environmen

Estimates from the Riverside Study of Sociocultural Factors

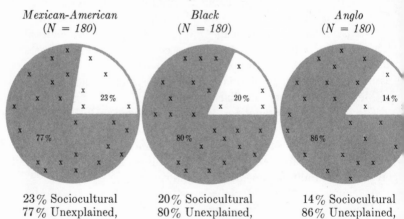

Mexican-American (N = 180)	Black (N = 180)	Anglo (N = 180)
23% Sociocultural 77% Unexplained, Includes Genotype	20% Sociocultural 80% Unexplained, Includes Genotype	14% Sociocultural 86% Unexplained, Includes Genotype

[a] Jensen, A. R. How much can we boost IQ and scholastic achievement? *Harvard Educational Review*, 1969, 39(1), 1–89.

Riverside study compared to Jensen's estimate of 70% to 80%. Thus, the within-ethnic-group estimates of the proportionate contribution of heredity and environment are approximately the same when using these two different approaches. It is possible that the correlations would have been higher in the Riverside data if other socio-cultural variables had been measured and measurements had been more reliable. No conclusions about between-group differences are possible using the kind of information depicted in Figure 1. There is no way to use heritability data collected on one ethnic group to explain the differences in average scores between ethnic groups, that is, average differences between the x's in the different circles.

Between-Ethnic-Group Differences

The second question concerning the influence of environmental factors on I.Q. test scores is that of accounting for between-ethnic-group differences in average test scores. Numerous studies have reported average I.Q. test scores which were between 10 and 15 points lower for Black and Mexican-American samples than for Anglo samples. The average Full Scale WISC I.Q. scores for the 180 Anglo children in our Riverside sample was 107.5 compared to 91.9 for the 180 Black children and 91.3 for the 180 Mexican-American. Differences in average Verbal I.Q. test scores were 105.5, 90.4, and 88.2, respectively. For Performance I.Q. they were 108.3, 92.8, and 96.3, respectively (see Table 1). Such differences are not surprising when we realize the Anglo-centric content of I.Q. tests, especially the verbal portions. However, the question still remains, "Can these differences be accounted for by the environmental, socio-cultural differences documented in Table 2 or are there other, perhaps genetic, factors also operating to produce the differences between the phenotypes of the three ethnic groups?"

THE HERITABILITY APPROACH

The "heritability" studies can deal only with the question of within-group differences because they estimate the percentage

89

of the variance among the I.Q. test scores of individuals which can be accounted for, statistically, by their biological relationship to each other. Ethnic groups, however, have highly independent lineage systems. There is no way, therefore, to estimate the percentage of the variance in individual test scores of persons from different ethnic groups which can be accounted for by the extent of their biological relationship to each other. Those who try to answer the question of between-group differences with data based on heritability studies are operating on faulty logic. The research design appropriate for answering the between-group question must be totally different from that needed to explain within-group differences.

CONCEPTUAL APPROACH APPROPRIATE
FOR EXPLAINING BETWEEN-GROUP DIFFERENCES

In an earlier analysis which included all the children in the larger sample ($N = 1513$), we developed a five item socio-cultural modality index based on family background characteristics and grouped Black and Mexican-American children according to the number of these characteristics in their background. Those with a score of five were children from families that corresponded to the mode for the Anglo community on all five characteristics; those with a score of four, corresponded to the mode on four characteristics; and so forth. For Mexican-American children the five items were: coming from less crowded families; having mothers who expected them to have some education beyond high school; having fathers who were reared in an urban environment (over 10,000 population) and who had a ninth grade education or more; living in a family which spoke English all or most of the time; and a family which owned or was buying its home. The five characteristics for Black children were: coming from a family with less than six members; having a mother who expected them to get some college education; having parents who were married and living together in a home which they owned or were buying; and having a father who had an occupation rated 30 or higher on the Duncan Socio-economic Index (Reiss, 1961).

The average I.Q. for the entire group of Mexican-American children was 90.4, approximately two-thirds of a standard deviation below the mean for the standardization group. The 127 children from backgrounds least like the modal socio-cultural configuration of the community, having 0 or only 1 modal characteristic, had an average I.Q. of 84.5. (This average is on the borderline of "mentally retarded," using the American Association of Mental Deficiency criterion.) The 146 children with 2 modal characteristics in their background had a mean I.Q. of 88.1, those with 3 modal characteristics had a mean I.Q. of 89.0, those with 4 modal characteristics had a mean I.Q. of 95.5, and those with all five modal characteristics had a mean I.Q. of 104.4. When social background was held constant there was no difference between the measured intelligence of Mexican-American and Anglo children.

The situation was just as dramatic for Black children. The total group of 339 Black children had an average I.Q. of 90.5 when there was no control for socio-cultural factors. The 47 children who came from backgrounds least like the modal configuration of the community had an average I.Q. of 82.7. Those with 2 modal characteristics had an average I.Q. of 87.1; those with 3 modal characteristics had an average I.Q. of 92.8; those with 4 modal characteristics had an average I.Q. of 95.5, and those with 5 characteristics had an average I.Q. of 99.5, exactly the national norm for the test. Thus, Black children who came from family backgrounds comparable to the modal pattern for the community did just as well on the Wechsler Intelligence Scale for Children as the children on whom the norms were based (Mercer, 1971b).

In the present paper, we have put the socio-cultural hypothesis to an even more rigorous test. We have attempted to determine if environmental factors can account, statistically, for the difference between the mean score of the Anglo children and that of the Mexican-American and Black children on all the I.Q. measures used in this study. For example, we are asking if environmental factors can explain the difference between the mean Full Scale WISC I.Q. of the 180 Anglo children in our sample (107.5) and the mean I.Q. of the 180 Black and the Mexican-

American children who had an average score of about 8 points below the norm for the test (91.9 and 91.3, respectively). This is a 16 point difference, slightly more than one standard deviation. The differential on the Verbal I.Q. is 17.3 points for Mexican-American and 15.1 points for Black respectively compared to Anglo children. The Performance I.Q. differential is 12.1 points for Mexican-American and 15.5 points for Black respectively compared to Anglo children. Differences on the Peabody Picture Vocabulary Test are 34.6 points for Mexican-American and 24.3 points for Black respectively compared to Anglo children!

Figure 2 presents a diagram to clarify, conceptually, the approach used in this analysis. We gave each child a score corresponding to the rank for the average Full Scale WISC I.Q. score of his ethnic group. Anglo children were scored 2 because their group had the highest average Full Scale WISC I.Q. Black children were each scored 1 because their average score fell in between and Mexican-American children were scored zero because their group had the lowest average score. The scores for ethnic group were correlated .47 with Full Scale WISC I.Q. when corrected for attenuation. Therefore, 22.1% of the differences between the individual I.Q. test scores of the 540 children in the three ethnic groups could be explained by differences in their ethnic group. This correlation estimates the maximum percentage of the variance which could be due to ethnic group.

The correlation between ethnic group and I.Q. test score is indicated by the broken arrow connecting ethnic group with I.Q. test score in Figure 2. The arrow is broken because we are hypothesizing that this correlation is a spurious relationship produced by the intervening effect of environmental factors, since the environmental variables which we have measured are not only correlated with I.Q. test score but are also correlated with ethnic group. The correlations between ethnic group and environmental factors are indicated by the solid arrows pointing upward in Figure 2. The correlations between environmental factors and I.Q. test score are indicated by the arrows pointing downward in Figure 2. If environmental factors are intervening

FIGURE 2 *Chart Depicting the Theoretical Model for Explaining Between-Ethnic-Group Differences on the Basis of Environmental Differences*

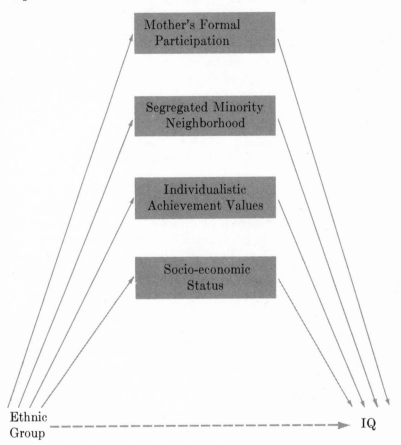

variables producing a spurious correlation between ethnic group and I.Q. test score, then we would hypothesize that when environmental factors are held constant, the correlation between ethnic group and I.Q. test score will approach zero, leaving little or no variance which could be due to ethnic group alone.

All correlations between socio-cultural factors and I.Q. test scores were linear for each ethnic group.

To test the hypothesis of spuriousness, we did a series of partial correlations between ethnic group and I.Q. test score for the 540 children in our three samples. All possible combinations of environmental factors were held constant to determine the most parsimonious explanation for the correlation between ethnic group and each of the measures of I.Q. Four environmental factors reduced the correlation to approximately zero for all three ethnic groups combined and Mexican-Americans vs Anglos: socio-economic status; individualistic achievement values; mother's formal participation; and living in a segregated minority neighborhood. All nine environmental factors were used in Black vs Anglo analyses. Table 4 presents our findings.

The first column in each set presents the correlation between ethnic group and various I.Q. measures when none of the environmental factors were held constant. The second column reports the partial correlation coefficient when environmental factors were held constant. The third column reports the percentage of variance still explained by ethnic group when environmental variables were held constant.

When environmental factors were held constant for all three ethnic groups taken together, there was no variance which could be explained by ethnic group alone except for a negligible 2.25% for the Peabody Picture Vocabulary Test. When each minority group was analyzed separately, the environmental measures in our data file were slightly more sensitive to the cultural characteristics of the Mexican-American than those of the Black sample. In spite of the fact that several socio-cultural measures were more appropriate for the Mexican-American than for the Black sample, the variance explained by ethnic group alone, after environmental factors had been controlled, was of little substantive importance for the Blacks—2.98% for Full Scale WISC I.Q.; .4% for Verbal I.Q.; and 4.84% for Performance I.Q.

The reason for the somewhat higher percentage of variance not accounted for by environmental factors on the Performance I.Q. in the Black vs Anglo analysis is apparent when we examine

94

TABLE 4 *Correlation Between Ethnic Group and Various I.Q. Measures With and Without Control for Environmental Factors*

I.Q. Test Used	All Groups (N = 540)			Black vs Anglo (N = 360)			Mexican-American vs Anglo (N = 360)		
	No Control Envirn. r	Control Envirn. $r_{(i.j)}$	Variance Explained by Ethnic Group %	No Control Envirn. r	Control Envirn. $r_{(i.j)}$	Variance Explained by Ethnic Group %	No Control Envirn. r	Control Envirn. $r_{(i.j)}$	Variance Explained by Ethnic Group %
WISC									
Full Scale I.Q.	.47	.00	.00	.56	.17	2.98	.56	.02	.04
Verbal I.Q.	.47	.00	.00	.46	.07	.49	.56	.01	.00
Performance I.Q.	.46	.00	.00	.55	.22	4.84	.44	.04	.16
Verbal Tests									
Information	.45	.00	.00	.43	.00	.00	.52	.00	.00
Comprehension	.30	.00	.00	.25	.00	.00	.36	.01	.01
Arithmetic	.31	.02	.04	.42	.14	1.96	.39	.00	.00
Similarities	.46	.06	.36	.44	.06	.36	.53	.06	.04
Vocabulary	.56	.06	.36	.50	.12	1.44	.31	.05	.01
Digit Span	.25	.01	.00	.31	.08	.64	.50	.13	1.69
Performance Tests									
Picture Completion	.29	.00	.00	.43	.13	1.69	.35	.00	.00
Picture Arrangement	.27	.00	.00	.39	.13	1.69	.33	.00	.00
Block Design	.31	.03	.09	.51	.26	6.76	.38	.05	.25
Coding	.24	.02	.04	.35	.05	.25	.29	.04	.16
Raven's Progressive Matrices	.32	.01	.00	.46	.13	1.69	.38	.04	.16
Peabody Picture Vocabulary	.68	.15	2.25	.63	.28	7.84	.77	.02	.04

the subtest findings. There is a correlation of .51 for the Block Design subtest when environmental factors are not controlled, which reduces to .26 when they are controlled. This leaves 6.76% of the original 26% of the variance still unexplained by the environmental indicators used in this study. The linear correlations between Block Design and Socio-economic Status and Individualistic Achievement Values, two primary, environmental variables in the analysis, are insignificant (r .04). It is not clear from our data why this particular subtest is not as highly correlated with these two environmental indicators as the other subtests in the WISC for Black children. These lower correlations are a factor in producing more unexplained variance for Block Design. They also produce a large percentage of unexplained variance for Performance I.Q. and, to a lesser extent, for Full Scale I.Q. Given the fact that over 300 correlations are involved in the various analyses presented in Table 4, some deviations from the overall pattern are to be expected.

It would be desirable to estimate, directly, how much of the original I.Q. point difference between the average test scores of the Anglo children and the average test scores of the Mexican-American and Black children in our sample still remained after controlling, statistically, for the environmental variables in our study. Unfortunately, an analysis of covariance, which would provide this information directly, is not appropriate for the kind of data we have in the study. However, for those subtests on which the explained variances is reduced to virtually zero, we know the I.Q. point difference is essentially zero. For those tests that have a small percentage of the variance still explained by ethnic group, the I.Q. point difference is probably quite small.

On the Peabody Picture Vocabulary Test, when all ethnic groups are analysed simultaneously, and there is no control for environmental factors, 46.2 percent of the variance in individual test scores can be accounted for by ethnic group. There is still almost 8% of the variance between Black and Anglo children explained by ethnic group after environmental factors are held constant. The poorest test in our study for any type of cross cultural comparison is, clearly, the Peabody Picture Vocabulary Test.

There are almost an infinite number of environmental indicators which could potentially be used to measure the socio-cultural isolation of Mexican-American and Black children from the core culture. If an investigator were designing a study specifically for this purpose, more sensitive measures than the ones available for this analysis could, undoubtedly, be devised. However, other indicators would probably produce roughly similar findings and the indicators used in this paper should not be interpreted as the specific "causes" of Mexican-American and Black children having lower I.Q. test scores. Because the environmental indicators are all highly intercorrelated, no attempt should be made to interpret which factor is most important. They should be regarded as a cluster of measures tapping more general socio-cultural differences which could have been measured using a variety of indicators.

Discussion

No set of empirical relationships is self explanatory. The social scientist, like any scientist, can construct a variety of explanatory theoretical models to account for a set of observed relationships. The problem is to select from among a given set of models the theoretical framework which provides the "best" explanatory scheme. Because this selection involves a value judgment, it is not likely that there will always be unanimous agreement on the "best" theory to explain any set of relationships. However, there are a set of generally accepted principles which guide the selection process.

First, if one model can explain the observed relationships with known and measured variables while another model requires postulating the operation of unknown and/or unmeasured variables, the model based on known, measured variables is to be preferred (Blalock, 1964).

Second, if one model is based on assumptions which have a higher level of probability of occurrence than another, the model with the higher level of probability is to be preferred to the model with the lower level of probability.

Third, when one model requires making more assumptions than another model, the model requiring the fewest assumptions is to be preferred as the most parsimonious.

Chance. One possible explanation for the relationships found in the present study is that they may result from chance factors peculiar to this particular sample of children, this particular group of measurements, or these specific data collection procedures. There is no reason to believe the children in the Riverside Public Schools differ significantly from children in other public school districts. However, the only way to examine this possibility is to replicate the study on other samples using similar procedures. A recent report of the National Center for Health Statistics presents findings similar to those of our study (Department of Health, Education, and Welfare Publication No. (HSM)72-1012). A representative sample of 7,119 children 6 through 11 years of age were examined using two subtests of the WISC, Block Design and Vocabulary, to estimate the child's I.Q. test score. Demographic data on family income, race, and education of the parents were obtained from one of the child's parents. White-Black differentials in mean score were approximately one standard deviation. In White-Black comparisons, the correlations between the race of the child and his scores on the test was .34 compared with a correlation of .56 in the present study. The correlation between I.Q. test score and education of parents was .48 and between I.Q. test score and family income was .43. These correlations are very close to those found in the present study between socio-economic status and Full Scale WISC I.Q., .51. When the effect of differences in education and family income was removed in the Public Health Service study, the association between race and I.Q. test score was reduced to .23. When socio-economic status was controlled in the Riverside study, the correlation between Full Scale I.Q. and

98

ethnic group was reduced to .35. In neither case were socio-economic factors, alone, sufficient to account entirely for ethnic differences in average I.Q. test scores. As we have seen, cultural as well as socio-economic factors need to be controlled. However, such a close replication of the Riverside findings on a national sample suggests that the relationships found in Riverside are not due entirely to some peculiarity of the samples used.

Unmeasured Genetic Factors. A second explanatory model might argue that uncontrolled and unmeasured genetic factors in the parents are, in fact, producing all of the observed relationships. This line of argument would go as follows: the genotype for "intelligence," that is, biological potential, of Mexican-American and Black parents is lower than that of Anglo parents. This hypothesized difference is inherited by the child and results in his phenotypic performance—lower I.Q. test score. This same unmeasured but assumed low biological potential results in Black and Mexican-American parents having lower occupational levels, completing less formal education, living in segregated minority neighborhoods, participating less in the formal organizations of the community, having a value system which places greater emphasis on family ties than on individualistic achievement, living in non-urbanized settings, having lower rates of home ownership, living more frequently in non-nuclear families, and having less familiarity with the English language and the American public school system. If this is the situation, then the relationships between ethnic group and the environmental factors measured in our study are spurious. Minority parents' low genetic potential is an intervening variable producing all of the observed relationships between I.Q. test scores, environmental characteristics, and ethnic group. Therefore, it would be hypothesized that the correlation between ethnic group and socio-cultural factors would approach zero, if parental genetic potential were held constant.

It should be noted, that it is always possible to argue that a set of observed relationships in any statistical analysis is, in fact, spurious because of the operation of some unmeasured factor. When this argument is made, however, the burden of proof rests with those hypothesizing the operation of the unmeasured factors rather than on those who are able to "explain" the relationship with known and measured variables (Blalock, 1964).

Although we feel that the burden of proof rests on those proposing the operation of an unmeasured genetic factor, we thought it would be interesting to attempt an indirect test of the hypothesis that the low biological potential of the parents is the primary reason for the disadvantaged position of Mexican-American and Black children. We cannot test this hypothesis of spuriousness directly because we do not have a measure of parental genotype, any more than we have a measure of the child's genotype. However, if we assume, as the heritability argument assumes, that the child's I.Q. test score is primarily genetic and is inherited from his parents, then we can use the child's I.Q. test score as an indirect measure of his parent's biological potential. Using the child's I.Q. test score as an indicator of his parent's I.Q. test scores, we can treat the I.Q. test score of the child as the intervening variable between ethnic group and environmental factors. According to the logic of this argument, if parental "intelligence" is controlled, then the correlation between each environmental variable and ethnic group should not only drop slightly, as a result of the environmental component which everyone admits is part of the I.Q. test score, but should approach zero.

Table 5 presents a series of partial correlations in which the child's Full Scale WISC I.Q. test score has been held constant when correlating ethnic group with the environmental variables used in our analysis. Although the correlations drop, the reductions are minimal and do not approach zero for any of the major variables in the study. There is still a large amount of unexplained variance when the genetic explanatory model is used.

The Socio-cultural Model. The third explanatory model regards the differences between the average I.Q. test scores of the children in the three ethnic groups as an artifact of the test, the population used in standardizing the test, and the cul-

100

TABLE 5 *Correlation Between Ethnic Group and the Eight Primary Sociocultural Variables Holding Full Scale WISC I.Q. Test Score Constant*

	Anglo-Mexican-American		Anglo-Black	
	No Control I.Q.	Control I.Q.	No Control I.Q.	Control I.Q.
	r	$r_{(i,j)}$	r	$r_{(i,j)}$
Socio-economic Status	.64	.50	.87	.80
Segregated Minority Neighborhood	.69	.57	.84	.77
Individualistic Achievement Values	.53	.39	.81	.71
Mother's Formal Participation	.26	.12	.47	.31
Cultural Barriers	−.54	−.39	−.65	−.51
Urbanization	.36	.29	.10	.10
Home Ownership	.39	.25	.27	.14
Family Structure	.29	.20	.10	.04

tural materials from which the test items were selected. This model concludes that the Mexican-American and Black children sampled in Riverside do not meet the assumptions of the inferential model for making between-group comparisons with Anglo children. Minority children have not had equivalent exposure to the materials covered in the test and do not come from backgrounds that equally value the individualistic achievement life style that is assumed in the timed, competitive nature of the test. Therefore, no valid inferences can be made from their phenotypic performance to their biological potential relative to the Anglo children sampled.

We hold that the socio-cultural explanatory framework is the most viable because it best meets the three criteria listed earlier. Firstly, the socio-cultural model explains the relationships between ethnic group and I.Q. test score, statistically, with known and measured variables. It does not require postulating the operation of some unmeasured variable.

Secondly, the socio-cultural model has a higher level of probability than the genetic model. The relationship between ethnic group and I.Q. approached zero when socio-cultural factors were controlled while the relationships between ethnic group and socio-cultural factors were only slightly reduced when the child's I.Q. test score was controlled.

Thirdly, the socio-cultural model requires making fewer untested assumptions. We know from this and other studies that both Mexican-American and Black children live under environmental circumstances which reduce their exposure to the Anglo core culture and the reasons for these circumstances can be explained historically. On the other hand, the genetic hypothesis requires making several assumptions which cannot be tested and which are highly improbable. It assumes that some unidentified genetic mechanism operates in both Black and Mexican-American populations to produce both their low I.Q. test scores and their socio-cultural characteristics. It assumes that this mechanism does not operate in the same fashion in the Anglo group. However, the Black and Mexican-American populations of Riverside are drawn from groups which have no history of intermarriage and could hardly share a common gene pool. In fact, both groups probably share more genes with the Anglo group than with each other. Sixty percent of the Black parents have moved into Riverside from the South since World War II and another twenty percent have migrated to Riverside from other parts of the United States since that time. One-third of the Mexican-American parents have themselves migrated from Mexico and the remaining parents are descended from families who migrated from Mexico since 1900. There were no mixed Mexican-American and Black marriages in our sample, although there were a few mixed minority-Anglo marriages. It seems highly improbable to assume that all of these phenotypic performances, which can be explained by known and measured socio-cultural circumstances, are, instead, determined genetically and, by chance, operate in two unrelated human populations but not in a third.

Therefore, we reject the genetic explanation of our findings and conclude that the differences in the average I.Q. tests scores for the children of the three ethnic groups in our sample are an artifact of the Anglo orientation and content of the test and result from differential exposure to the cultural materials covered in the items. When socio-cultural variables are held constant, the unaccounted for residual variance which can be attributed to ethnic group alone approaches zero. What little residual variance remains unexplained could be due to errors of measurement and/or to the omission of other unmeasured socio-cultural factors from the analysis.

Conclusions

We concluded from our analysis that approximately 20% of the observed differences between the I.Q. test scores of children of the same ethnic group can be explained by differences in their socio-cultural backgrounds. The 80% of the variance which is unexplained includes genetic factors but may also include some socio-cultural factors not measured by our indicators. We were able to identify five socio-cultural groups within both the Black and Mexican-American samples which had mean I.Q.s ranging over 15 points. With this amount of variance due to environment, even children of the same ethnic group do not meet the assumptions of the inferential model and no inferences should be drawn about their relative biological potential without controlling for sociocultural differences within ethnic group.

We also concluded from our findings that the differences between the average I.Q. test scores of children from the three different ethnic groups we studied could be explained, statistically, by differences in their environmental backgrounds. Children from the three ethnic groups do not meet the assumptions of the inferential model. Therefore, theories of intelligence which postulate ethnic differences in biological potential on the basis of differences in mean I.Q. test scores are erroneously interpreting socio-cultural differences as biological differences.

"Intelligence" Testing vs "Achievement" Testing

Binet chose to call his original test for identifying children who were not likely to succeed in the regular academic program of the schools an "intelligence" test. Subsequently, others who have developed similar tests have followed his lead and have also called their measures tests of "intelligence."

Paralleling the development of "intelligence" tests has been the development of tests intended to measure academic achievement in specific subject areas. Such tests, at the elementary school level, usually focus on reading and mathematical skills. The two types of tests are, presumably, different in that tests of academic achievement are supposedly more culture bound and more heavily dependent upon school instruction than measures of "intelligence." Eysenck takes this position in his recent book *The I.Q. Argument: Race, Intelligence, and Education.* 'He argues that tests used in typical educational selection (such as the 11+ exams in England) are clearly not culturally fair and "are *not* meant to be universally valid, nor to give as pure a measure of I.Q. as could be obtained." They are at the "culturally determined" end of the continuum, while "pure I.Q. tests" are at the other, "culture fair", end of the continuum (Eysenck, 1971, p. 52). Jensen also justifies making a psychological distinction between "intelligence" tests and "achievement" tests. He argues that achievement tests sample "very narrowly from the most specifically taught skills in the traditional curriculum" while "intelligence" tests sample "from a very wide range of potential experiences" which "gets at the learning that occurs in the total life experience of the individual." He then contends that environmental factors make a much larger contribution to individual differences in achievement scores than to individual differences in I.Q. test scores.

\ Persons who claim that I.Q. tests and achievement tests are psychologically distinct tend to "explain" performance on achievement tests as a function of "intelligence" that is, I.Q. test score. I.Q. test score is regarded as the "input" variable and academic achievement score is regarded as the "output" variable. Using this type of reasoning, they conclude that the public schools can do relatively little to improve the academic achievement of Black and Mexican-American children because their "intelligence" and their family background, together, can account, statistically, for their lower academic achievement. [If, however, the distinction between "I.Q." test and "achievement" test is not valid and the two tests are, in fact, both equally sensitive to socio-cultural factors, and measuring essentially the same characteristics, then

104

the argument that minority children have low academic achievement because they have low "intelligence" becomes highly circular, a mere tautology.

A factor analysis is frequently used to determine if tests are measuring different dimensions. Jensen reports the results of a factor analysis of measures of achievement and measures of "intelligence" given a sample of public school children in the state of California. After ascertaining that Anglo, Black and Mexican-American samples yielded similar factors, he combined all three groups for an overall factor analysis. Factor I consisted of measures of scholastic achievement and a measure of verbal intelligence. Factor loadings were higher for older than younger children and ranged from .58 to .89. Achievement test scores did not factor separately from measures of "verbal intelligence" (Jensen, 1971). Such findings are usually interpreted to mean the measures loading on the same factors are not psychologically distinct.

We approached the question of the socio-cultural component of achievement tests as compared with I.Q. tests from the perspective used in our earlier analysis. Fortunately, our data files contained reading achievement scores for all the children in our samples on tests given within one year of the time the I.Q. tests were administered. Children in grades 1 through 3 took Stanford Achievement Tests and those in grades 4 through 6 took the Sequential Test of Educational Progress (STEP). We developed local norms based on the performance of all the children in the school district on each of the tests at each grade level for the year prior to our study. These standard scores had a mean of 50 and a standard deviation of 10. The score of each child in our sample was then transformed into a standard score, relative to the district norms. The average reading achievement score for the Anglo children in our sample was 52.8. The average for the Mexican-American children was 44.3 and the average for the Black children 44.9. The difference between the mean score of the Anglo children and that of the minority children is about one standard deviation, approximately the same magnitude as for differences in mean I.Q. test scores.

We did multiple correlations using reading achievement as the dependent variable and the nine socio-cultural variables as independent variables to determine the percentage of the variance in reading achievement within ethnic group that could be accounted for by differences in socio-cultural background factors. The multiple correlation coefficients were as follows: Anglo children, .43 (18.7% of the variance); Black children, .42 (17.3% of the variance); and Mexican-American children, .51 (26.2% of the variance). These correlations are of approximately the same magnitude as the correlations between socio-cultural factors and I.Q. tests scores. (See Table 3.) We cannot say that one type of test is substantially more "cultural fair" than the other.

We also did a series of partial correlations in which the child's reading achievement was treated as the dependent variable and ethnic group was coded "2" for Anglo "1" for Black and "0" for Mexican-American children, the rank order of their mean reading achievement scores. The correlation between ethnic group and reading achievement, corrected for attenuation, was .39, slightly lower than the correlation between ethnic group and Full Scale WISC I.Q., .47. When socio-cultural factors were held constant, the correlation between ethnic group and reading achievement dropped to .008, leaving no variance explained by the ethnic group alone. When the Black children were compared to the Anglo children, the correlation without socio-cultural control was .44. Controlling socio-cultural factors, it was .09 leaving less than 1% of the variance explained by ethnic group alone. When the Mexican-American children were compared to the Anglo children, the correlation without socio-cultural control was .45. With controls, the correlation dropped to .01, leaving less than 1% of the variance explained by ethnic group. In short, the difference in the mean reading achievement scores of children of different ethnic groups, like differences in mean I.Q. test scores, could be explained, statistically, by differences in their socio-cultural background. Mayeske reported similar findings when he analyzed the Coleman data and partialed out socio-cultural factors in achievement comparing Caucasian, Black, Mexican-American, Puerto Rican, American Indian and Asian American children. (Mayeske, 1971).

Finally, we correlated the reading achievement of children of each ethnic group with their WISC I.Q. test scores and found the following correlations: Full Scale WISC I.Q.—.56 for Anglo, .55 for Black, .62 for Mexican-American children; Verbal I.Q.—.54 for Anglo, .53 for Black, .60 for Mexican-American children; and Performance I.Q.—.45 for Anglo, .46 for Black and .50 for Mexican-American children. These correlations are of approximately the *same* magnitude as the correlations of the subtests of the WISC with Full Scale WISC I.Q., Verbal I.Q., and Performance I.Q. for $7\frac{1}{2}$ year old children (Wechsler, 1949). Reading achievement scores appear to be no more psychologically distinct from WISC I.Q. test scores than are the subtests of the WISC itself. We concluded from our analysis that reading achievement scores cannot be distinguished from I.Q. test scores either by their socio-cultural component or their correlations with measures of "intelligence."

Implications of Findings for Educational Planning

A strong case has been made for abandoning the I.Q. test in educational placement and planning. This case rests on two basic contentions, both readily documented in educational practice.

The first is based on the socio-cultural argument pursued in this paper. Although the cultural biases in I.Q. tests have been recognized since the 1930's, they are seldom, if ever, taken into account in assessing individual performance. Socio-cultural biases are not emphasized and, usually, are not even discussed in the training of psychometrists and school psychologists. Relatively few psychologists pay any attention to the inferential model on which valid inferences must be based, except when evaluating physically disabled or emotionally disturbed persons. Although the major I.Q. tests now being used in the public schools were not designed for or standardized on Black, Mexican-American, Puerto Rican, American Indian, or other minority groups within American society and are clearly not culturally appropriate for large segments of these populations, they have been used to assess, label, and classify persons from these populations as mentally retarded, slow learners, basic students, and so forth. This Anglocentric process is so highly institutionalized in American public schools that identical patterns of labeling and placement appear in every region of the country where there are disadvantaged and/or non-Anglo populations.

The net effect of this near universal process has been to assign many minority children to limited educational programs and to shift responsibility for the educational failure of minority children from the schools to the individual child and his family. If the school fails to educate a group of minority children and the school can show that these minority children have a low average I.Q. test score, then the school has been able to absolve itself of the responsibility for their academic deficiencies by interpreting these low test scores as a sign of low biological potential. The schools cannot be expected to change biology and little has been done to develop appropriate educational programs for minority children.

On the other hand, if the low average I.Q. test score of minority children results, primarily, from lack of exposure to the Anglo core culture, then the school cannot absolve itself of its educational responsibility. It must develop programs which build upon the cultural backgrounds of minority children and it must assume responsibility for their education and for bringing them into the mainstream of American life. The interpretation of the I.Q. test score as a measure of "mental ability" has been, historically, a serious impediment to the development of programs geared to the cultural backgrounds of minority children. So long as the schools could maintain, in good conscience, that a group of children were not fully educable, the educators in the schools need not feel guilty for not fully educating them. This is exactly what has happened as a result of the naive interpretation of I.Q. test scores as measures of biological potential, that is, "intelligence." Abandoning I.Q. tests would, in one sweeping act, eliminate the misinterpretation and misuse of I.Q. tests in educational practice by making I.Q. test scores unavailable and irrelevant. Abolishing I.Q. testing would force educators to look beyond the I.Q. label and come to grips with the needs of individual children in all their individual, socio-cultural complexity.

A second argument for abandoning the I.Q. test is that the kind of scores and information provided by present tests are of little practical value to the educator. Even when properly interpreted, scores are not very helpful in educational planning. They do not tell a teacher how well a Mexican-American child understands spoken English so she can assess his need for special instruction in English as a second language. They do not tell her his reading level, his proficiency in math, or provide the basic information needed to make the day-to-day decisions in planning for a child's education. In their present form, I.Q. tests add little to the educational process.

In spite of the cogency of these arguments, we have taken a more moderate position based on the assumption that there is some value in knowing how well children are doing in relation to their age peers so that those children who need supplementary educational programs can be identified and assisted. We believe that that problem is not in the tests themselves but in the way test scores have been interpreted and used. We believe it is possible to educate persons to think in terms of the inferential model presented in this paper and to use test information in a socially constructive and educationally sound fashion. However, such an effort will not be successful unless certain fundamental changes are made in the way in which we think about test scores.

Firstly, we feel that too many professional and lay persons have come to believe Binet's label and actually regard test scores as measures of "native intelligence." For this reason, we believe that the names attached to these tests should be changed. Instead of measures of "intelligence" or "mental ability," they should be labeled to indicate more accurately what they are actually measuring—general academic readiness. Present tests provide a global prediction of which children are likely to succeed in the regular program of an American public school without supplementary help. Thus, they are of some value in identifying those children who will need special, supplementary educational programs. However, they do not indicate in any detail what kind of supplementary educational programs should be provided. Additional, more refined measures are needed for actual program planning and prescriptive teaching.

Secondly, we believe that the scores from such tests should not be referred to as "I.Q.," that is, "intelligence quotients." The notion that these scores result from the relationship between chronological age and mental age is archaic. I.Q. test scores on most major tests are no longer "quotients" at all. They are simply the average score of a particular age group in the standardization sample set to 100 with a standard deviation set to 15. They are called "intelligence quotients," in deference to an outmoded tradition. The term "I.Q.," has acquired a semi-mystical meaning which renders it almost useless as a scientific construct and leads to such nonsense as attempts to differentiate between tests of "verbal reasoning" and "pure I.Q. tests." Shifting the base to some number other than 100 such as 50 or 500, and changing the standard deviation to 10 or 100 would help break up such faulty gestalts and provide a fresh start. In addition, reporting scores as profiles and in the form of percentile bands rather than as single numbers would be salutary. This procedure is, of course, already used with most standard tests.

Thirdly, and most importantly, we believe that normative frameworks need to be developed for each of the major ethnic and cultural groups in American society so that a child's performance on any standardized test can be compared with that of other children from similar socio-cultural backgrounds. This procedure would bring us closer to meeting the assumptions of the inferential model described in this paper. If a child scores below the general population norms for the test but scores within the normal range for his socio-cultural group, he would not be regarded as subnormal. Instead, he would be treated as a

110

child from a socio-cultural background that differs from the Anglo cultural mode and who has not had the opportunity to acquire the knowledge and skills needed to achieve in the dominant society. He would be given educational programs specifically designed to close the socio-cultural gap and prepare him for participation in the mainstream of American life. Such pluralistic, socio-culturally sensitive interpretations of the meaning of children's performances on all types of standardized tests would provide a much sounder basis for educational decision-making than is now possible with a single Anglo norm. With such norms, present tests could be made more educationally relevant. Such procedures would more nearly reflect the rich cultural variety of American life. They would counteract the tendency to oversimplify the interpretive process by making naive genetic interpretations of complex socio-cultural phenomena.

REFERENCES

Altus, W. D. The American-Mexican: The survival of a culture. *Journal of Social Psychology*. 1949, *29*, 210–220.

Blalock, H. M. *Causal inferences in nonexperimental research*. Chapel Hill; University of North Carolina Press, 1964.

Binet, A., & Simon T. Sur la necessite d'establir un diagnostic scientifique des etats inferieurs de l'intelligence *Annee Psychologique*. 1905, *11*, 1–28.

Buros, O. I. (Ed.) *The sixth mental measurements yearbook*. Highland Park, New Jersey: Gryphon Press, 1965.

Burt, C. The genetic determination of differences in intelligence: A study of monozygotic twins reared together and apart. *British Journal of Psychology*. 1966, *57*, 137–153.

Darcy, N. T. "Bilingualism and the measurement of intelligence: Review of a decade of research" *Journal of Genetic Psychology*. 1963, *103*, 259–282.

Dunn, L. M. Expanded manual, *Peabody Picture Vocabulary Test*. Minneapolis: American Guidance Service Inc., 1965.

Eells, K. et al., *Intelligence and cultural differences*. Chicago: University of Chicago Press, 1951.

111

Eysenck, H. J. *The I.Q. argument: Race, intelligence, and education.* New York: The Library Press, 1971.

Gordon, M. M. *Assimilation in American life.* New York: Oxford University Press, 1964, 72–76.

Guilford, J. P. *Fundamental statistics in psychology and education.* New York: McGraw Hill, 1965.

Herrnstein, R. I.Q. *The Atlantic Monthly.* September, 1971, 43–64.

Lenski, G. *The religious factor.* New York: Doubleday & Co., 1961.

Jensen, A. R. How much can we boost I.Q. and scholastic achievement? *Harvard Educational Review.* Vol. 39, No. 1, Winter, 1969, 1–123.

Jensen, A. R. Do schools cheat minority children? *Education Research,* November, 1971.

Lord, F. M. A paradox in the interpretation of group comparisons. *Psychological Bulletin.* Vol. 68, No. 5, 1969, 304–305.

Mayeske, G. W. On *The explanation of racial-ethnic group differences in achievement test scores.* Paper presented for American Psychological association meetings, Washington, D.C., September, 1971.

Mercer, J. R. Sociological perspectives on mild mental retardation: In H. Carl Haywood (Ed.) *Social-cultural aspects of mental retardation: Proceeding of the Peabody NIMH Conference.* New York: Appleton-Century-Crafts, Inc., 1970.

Mercer, J. R. Sociocultural factors in labeling mental retardates. *The Peabody Journal of Education.* April, 1971, 48(3), 188.

Mercer, J. R. Institutionalized Anglocentrism: Labeling mental retardates in the public schools. In Peter Orleans and William R. Eliss Jr. (Ed.) *Race, change, and urban society.* Urban Affairs Annual Review, Vol. V., Los Angeles: Sage Publications, Inc., 1971.

Mercer, J. R. Who is normal? Two perspectives on mild mental retardation. *Patients, physicians and illness* (Rev. ed.) E. G. Jaco, (Ed.) New York: The Free Press of Glencoe, 1972.

Mercer, J. R. *Labeling the mentally retarded.* Berkeley: University of California Press, 1972, in press.

Racial and ethnic survey of California public schools, Part I: Distribution of pupils, Fall, 1966, 1967, 1968, Sacramento: State Department of Education, 1966, 1967, 1968.

Raven, J. C. *Guide to the standard progressive matrices.* London: H. K. Lewis & Co., Ltd., 1960.

Reiss, A. *Occupations and social status.* New York: The Free Press, 1961.

Sarason, S.; Davidson, K.; Lighthall, F.; Waite, R.; Ruebush, B.; *Anxiety in elementary school children.* New York: John Wiley & Son, 1960.

Srole, L. Social integration and certain corollaries: An explanatory study. *American Sociological Review.* 1956, Vol. 21, 709–716.

Strodtbeck, F. L. Family interaction, values and achievement in A. L. Baldwin, Urie Bronfenbrenner, D. C. McClelland, J. L. Strodtbeck. *Talent and society.* Princeton, New Jersey: D. Van Nostrand, 1958.

Terman, L. M., & Merrill, M. A. *Stanford-Binet intelligence scale.* Boston: Houghton Mifflin, 1960.

Turner, R. *The social context of ambition.* San Francisco: Chandler Publishing Co., 1964.

U.S. Censuses of population and housing: 1960 *Final report PHI(1)-135, census tract, San Bernardino-Riverside-Ontario, California standard metropolitan statistical area.* Washington, D.C.: U.S. Government Printing Office, 1962.

U.S. Department of Health, Education and Welfare, *Public Health Service, vital and health statistics, series 11-number 110.* "Intellectual development of children by demographic and socioeconomic factors United States" Washington, D.C.: U.S. Government Printing Office, December, 1971.

Wechsler, D. *WISC manual, Wechsler intelligence scale for children.* New York: The Psychological Corporation, 1949.

Wechsler, D. *The measurement and appraisal of adult intelligence.* (4th ed.) Baltimore: Williams & Wilkins, 1958.

113

6

SCIENCE OR SUPERSTITION?
(A Physical Scientist Looks
at the I.Q. Controversy)

BY DAVID LAYZER

That valid judgments about the biological significance of differences in tests of mental abilities are impossible has already been stressed in preceding sections. This is a point that cannot be over-emphasized in view of the immediacy of the racial problems confronting the United States at this time. Various proposals have been advanced by probably well-intentioned people that suggest how meaningful investigation of genetic rather than phenotypic differences in intelligence and achievement might be carried out. Most of these individuals suffer from the obstinate inability to see the methodological difficulties and inherent biases of their schemes. Some anthropologists even opine that such studies are irrelevant or too vulnerable to misinterpretation and too fraught with political danger to be undertaken. This may or may not be true, but it is a fact that generations of discrimination have made direct comparisons of mental traits between Negroes and whites not biologically meaningful.

—I. M. Lerner (1968, p. 234)

A number of years ago, when high school teachers in North Carolina were being paid a starting salary of $120 per month, I happened to ask a member of that state's legislature whether he considered this to be an adequate salary. "Certainly," he said, "they're not worth any more than that." "How do you know?" I asked. "Why, just look at what they're paid." Circular reasoning? I think not. Our views on salary and status reflect our basic assumptions concerning the individual and his relation to society. One possible assumption is that society should reward each of its members according to his needs and contributions. Another is that society has a fixed hierarchic structure and each individual gravitates inevitably toward the level where he belongs. My question was based on the first assumption, the legislator's reply on the second.

The idea that, by and large, we get what we deserve—that there is a pre-ordained harmony between what we are and what we achieve—was an essential ingredient in the Calvinist doctrine of New England's Puritan settlers. What really mattered to them was not, of course, how well they did in this world but how well they would do in the next. The first was important only insofar as it provided a clue to the second. Although Calvinism's other-worldly orientation has long since gone out of fashion, its underlying social attitudes persist and continue to play an important part in shaping our social, educational and political institutions. Because we still tend to interpret wealth and power as tokens of innate worth (and poverty and helplessness as tokens of innate worthlessness), we tend to believe that it is wicked to tamper with "natural" processes of selection and rejection (Thou shalt not monkey with the Market), to erect artificial barriers against economic mobility (downward or upward), or to penalize the deserving rich in order to benefit the undeserving poor.

Not unnaturally, such attitudes have always appealed strongly to the upwardly mobile and those who already inhabit society's upper strata. Besides, they offer a convenient rationalization for our failure to cope with, or even to confront, our most urgent social problem: the emergence of a growing and self-perpetuating lower class, disproportionately Afro- and Latin-American in its ethnic composition, excluded from the mainstream of American life and alienated from its values, isolated in rural areas and urban ghettos, and dependent for the means of bare survival on an increasingly hostile and resentful majority. Faced with this problem, many people find it comforting to believe that human nature, not the System, is responsible for gross inequalities in the human condition. As Richard Nixon has said, "Government could provide health, housing, means, and clothing for all Americans. That would not make us a great country. What we have to remember is that this country is going to be great in the future to the extent that individuals have self-respect, pride and a determination to do better."

Although such attitudes are deeply ingrained, increasing numbers of Americans are beginning to question their validity. The System may be based on eternal moral truths, but in practice it seems to be working less and less well; and one of the eternal moral truths does, after all, assert that practical success is inner virtue's outward aspect. Yet the quality of life in America is deteriorating in many ways, not only for the downwardly mobile lower class (who, according to Mr. Nixon, are not trying hard enough) but also for the upwardly mobile middle class (who are already trying as hard as they can). In these circumstances any argument that lends support to the old, embattled attitudes is bound to arouse strong emotional responses both among those who recognize a need for basic social reform and among those who oppose it.

JENSENISM

This may help to explain the furor generated by the publication, in a previously obscure educational journal, of a long scholarly article provocatively entitled, "How Much Can We Boost I.Q. and Scholastic Achievement?" (Jensen 1969). Very little, concludes the author, because differences in I.Q. largely reflect innate differences in intelligence. Children with low I.Q.'s, he argues, lack the capacity to acquire specific cognitive skills, namely, those involved in abstract reasoning and problem solving. Such children should be taught mainly by rote and should not be encouraged to aspire to occupations that call for higher cognitive skills.

What is true of individuals could also well be true of groups, continues Jensen: differences between ethnic groups in average performance on I.Q. tests probably reflect average differences

116

in innate intellectual capacity. Jensen does not shirk the unpleasant duty of pointing out that this conclusion has an important bearing on fundamental questions of educational, social and political policy:—

Since much of the current thinking behind civil rights, fair employment, and equality of educational opportunity appeals to the fact that there is a disproportionate representation of different racial groups in the various levels of educational, occupational and socioeconomic hierarchy, we are forced to examine all the possible reasons for the inequality among racial groups in the attainments and rewards generally valued by all groups within our society. To what extent can such inequalities be attributed to unfairness in society's multiple selection processes? . . . And to what extent are these inequalities attributable to really relevant selection criteria which apply equally to all individuals but at the same time select disproportionately between some racial groups because there exist, in fact, real average differences among the groups—differences . . . indisputably relevant to educational and occupational performance?

The contention that I.Q. is an index of innate cognitive capacity is, of course, not new, but it has not been taken very seriously by most biologists and psychologists. Jensen's article purports to put it on a sound scientific basis. In outline, his argument runs as follows. I.Q. test scores represent measurements of a human trait which we may call intelligence. It is irrelevant to the argument that we do not know what intelligence "really is." All that we need to know is that I.Q. tests are internally and mutually consistent and that I.Q. correlates strongly with scholastic success, income, occupational status, etc. We can then treat I.Q. as if it was a metric character like height or weight, and use techniques of population genetics to estimate its "heritability." In this way we can discover the relative importance of genetic and environmental differences as they contribute to differences in I.Q. Such studies show, according to Jensen, that I.Q. differences are approximately 80% genetic in origin. Jensen's 123-page article is largely devoted to fleshing out this argument and developing its educational implications. Jensenism has also been expounded at a more popular level: in Great Britain by H. J. Eysenck (1971) and in America by R. J. Herrnstein (1971). While Eysenck's main concern is to stress the genetic basis of differences between ethnic groups, Herrnstein is more concerned with the social and political implications of Jensenism. He argues that the more successful we are in our efforts to equalize opportunity and environment, the more closely will the structure of society come to reflect inborn differences in mental ability. Thus "our present social policies" must inevitably give rise to a hereditary caste system based largely on I.Q. Indeed, the lowest socio-economic classes *already* consist of people with the lowest I.Q.'s. Since, according to Jensen, I.Q. is essentially genetically determined, Herrnstein's argument implies that the current inhabitants of urban ghettos and depressed rural areas are destined to become the progenitors of a hereditary caste, its members, doomed by their genetic incapacity to do well on I.Q. tests, to remain forever unemployed and unemployable, a perpetual burden and a perpetual threat to the rest of society.

Many of Jensen's and Herrnstein's critics have accused them of social irresponsibility. In reply, Jensen and Herrnstein have invoked the scholar's right to pursue and publish the truth without fear or favor. Besides, they point out, we cannot escape the consequences of unpleasant truths either by shutting our eyes to them or by denouncing them on ideological grounds. But how firmly based are these "unpleasant truths"?

The educational, social and political implications of Jensen's doctrine justify a careful examination of this question. It is easy to react emotionally to Jensenism, but teachers and others who help to shape public attitudes toward education and social policy cannot allow themselves to be guided wholly by their emotional responses to this issue.

There is another reason why Jensen's technical argument repays analysis. It exemplifies—almost to the point of caricature—a research approach that is not uncommon in the social sciences. Taking the physical sciences as their putative model, the practitioners of this approach eschew metaphysical speculation and work exclusively with hard, preferably numerical, data, from which they seek to extract objective and quantitative laws. Thus Jensen deduces from statistical analyses of I.Q. test scores that 80% of the variance in these scores (the average value of the *squares* of the differences between individual test scores and their average) is attributable to genetic differences. By exposing in some detail the logical and methodological fallacies underlying Jensen's analysis, I hope to draw attention to the weaknesses inherent in the "operational" approach that it exemplifies.

THE IRRELEVANCE OF HERITABILITY

Jensen's central contention, and the basis for his and Herrnstein's doctrines on education, race and society, is that the heritability of I.Q. is about .8. This means that about 80% of the variance in I.Q. among, say, Americans of European descent is attributable to genetic factors. Other authors have made other estimates of the heritability of I.Q.—some higher, some considerably lower than .8. In the following pages I shall try to explain why all such estimates are unscientific and indeed meaningless. But before we embark on a discussion of heritability theory and its applicability to human intelligence, it is worth noticing that, even if Jensen's central contention were meaningful and valid, it would not have the implications that he and others have drawn from it. Suppose for the sake of the argument that I.Q. was a measure of some metric trait like height, and that it had a high heritability. This would mean that under prevailing developmental conditions, variations in I.Q. are due largely to genetic differences between individuals. It would tell us nothing, however, about what might happen under different developmental conditions. Suppose—to take a more concrete example than I.Q.—that a hypothetical population of first-graders raised in identical environments has been taught to read by method A. Measured differences in their reading ability would still have been attributable largely to genetic factors, but both the individual scores on a test of reading ability, and even their rank

119

order might have been quite different, since it is well known that different methods of teaching reading suit different children. Thus, *the heritability of such scores tells us nothing about the educability of the children being tested.* To conclude, as Jensen and Herrnstein have done, that children with low I.Q.'s have a relatively low capacity for acquiring certain cognitive skills is to assume either that these skills cannot be taught at all or that, insofar as they can be taught, they have been taught equally well to all children.

What does the alleged high heritability of I.Q. imply about genetic differences between ethnic groups? The answer to this question is unequivocal: nothing. Geneticists have been pointing out for well over half a century that it is meaningless to try to separate genetic and environmental contributions to measured differences between different stocks bred under different developmental conditions. Between ethnic groups, as between socioeconomic groups, there are systematic differences in developmental conditions (physical, cultural, linguistic, etc.) known to influence performance on I.Q. tests substantially. Since we have no way of correcting test scores for these differences, the only objectively correct statement that can be made on this subject is that "the reported differences in average I.Q. tell us nothing whatever about any average genetic differences that may exist. On the data, black genetic superiority in intelligence (or whatever it is that I.Q. tests measure) is neither more nor less likely than white superiority." Professor Herrnstein appears to have misunderstood this point: he writes that the reported differences between ethnic groups could be "more genetic, less genetic, or precisely as genetic as implied by a heritability of .8." If we ultimately succeed in building a color-blind society, then and only then will we be able to estimate, in retrospect, how great the systematic effects of racial prejudice really were. As S. L. Washburn (quoted by Lerner 1968) has said,

> I am sometimes surprised to hear it stated
> that if Negroes were given an equal opportunity,
> their I.Q. would be the same as the whites'. If

one looks at the degree of social discrimination
against Negroes and their lack of education,
and also take into account the tremendous amount
of overlapping between the observed I.Q.'s of
both, one can make an equally good case that,
given a comparable chance to that of the whites,
their I.Q.'s would test out ahead. Of course,
it would be absolutely unimportant in a democratic society if this were to be true, because
the vast majority of individuals of
both groups would be of comparable intelligence,
whatever the mean of these intelligence tests would show.

To sum up, even if Jensen's considerations of the heritability
of I.Q. were meaningful and valid, they would have no direct
bearing on the question of educability or on the issue of genetic
differences between ethnic groups. Their apparent relevance is
a result of semantic confusion. In ordinary usage, when we speak
of a highly heritable trait we mean one that is largely inborn.
In genetics, however, a trait can have high heritability either
because its expression is insensitive to environmental variation
or because the range of relevant environmental variation happens to be small. Jensen and Herrnstein apparently assume that
the first of these alternatives is appropriate for I.Q. But the
available experimental evidence, some of which is cited later
in this article, shows that I.Q. scores are in fact highly sensitive
to variations in relevant developmental conditions.

SCIENCE AND SCIENTISM: A QUESTION OF METHODOLOGY

The theory of heritability, some elementary aspects of which
are described below, was developed by geneticists within a well-
defined biological context. The theory applies to metric characters of plants and animals—height, weight and the like. To apply
this theory to human intelligence, Jensen and the authors whose
work he summarizes must assimilate intelligence to a metric
character and I.Q. to a measurement of that character. Most
biologists would, I think, hesitate to take this conceptual leap.

121

Jensen, however, justifies it on the following philosophical grounds:—

> Disagreements and arguments can perhaps be forestalled if we take an operational stance. First of all, this means that probably the most important fact about intelligence is that we can measure it. Intelligence, like electricity, is easier to measure than to define. And if the measurements bear some systematic relationships to other data, it means we can make meaningful statements about the phenomenon we are measuring. There is no point in arguing the question to which there is no answer, the question of what intelligence *really* is. The best we can do is obtain measurements of certain kinds of behavior and look at their relationships to other phenomena and see if these relationships make any kind of sense and order. It is from these orderly relationships that we gain some understanding of the phenomena.

The "operational stance" recommended by Jensen is thought by many social scientists to be the key ingredient in the "scientific method" as practised by physical scientists. This belief is mistaken. The first and most crucial step toward an understanding of any natural phenomenon is not measurement. One must begin by deciding which aspects of the phenomenon are worth examining. To do this intelligently, one needs to have, at the very outset, some kind of explanatory or interpretive framework. In the physical sciences this framework often takes the form of a mathematical theory. The quantities that enter into the theory—mass, electric charge, force, and so on—are always much easier to define than to measure. They are, in fact, completely—if implicitly—defined through the equations that make up the theory.

Once a mathematical theory has been formulated, its predictions can be compared with observation or experiment. This requires appropriate measurements. The aspect of scientific measurements that non-scientists most often fail to appreciate is that they always presuppose a theoretical framework. Even exploratory measurements, carried out before one has a definite theory to test, always refer to quantities that are precisely defined within a broader theoretical context. For example, although we do not yet have a theory for the origin of cosmic rays, we know that such a theory must involve the masses, energies, momenta and charges of cosmic-ray particles. In designing apparatus to measure these quantities, physicists use well-established mathematical theories that describe the behavior of fast particles under a wide variety of conditions. The theoretical framework for a given set of measurements may be wrong, in which case the measurements will ultimately lead to inconsistencies, but it must not be vague. In short, significant measurements usually grow from theories, not vice versa. Jensen's views on scientific method derive not from the practice of physical scientists but from the philosophical doctrine of Francis Bacon (1561–1626), who taught that meaningful generalizations emerge spontaneously from systematic measurements.

These considerations apply equally to biology, where mathematical theories do not yet occupy the commanding position they do in the physical sciences. The following criticism by C. H. Waddington (1957) of *conventional* applications of the heritability theory is illuminating:—

> . . . There has been a tendency to regard a refined statistical analysis of incomplete experiments as obviating the necessity to carry the experiments further and to design them in more penetrating fashion. For instance, if one takes some particular phenotypic character such as body weight or milk yield, one of the first steps in an analysis of its genetic basis should be to try to break down the underlying physiological systems into a number of more or less independent factors. Are some genes affecting the milk yield by increasing the quantity of secreting tissue, others by affecting the efficiency of secretion, and others in still other ways?

These views contrast sharply with those of Jensen and Herrnstein, who believe in the possibility of discovering meaningful relations between measurable aspects of human behavior without inquiring too closely into the biological or psychological significance of that behavior. In this way they hope to avoid "metaphysical" speculation. This is an admirable objective. But it is not so easy to operate without a conceptual framework. As we shall see, what Jensen and Herrnstein have in fact done is not to dispense with metaphysical assumptions but to dispense with stating them. Such a policy is especially dangerous in the social sciences, where experimental verification of hypotheses is usually difficult or impossible. As Gunnar Myrdal has wisely pointed out, the failure of the social sciences to achieve the same degree of objectivity as the natural sciences can be attributed, at least as much, to a persistent neglect on the part of social scientists to state and examine their basic assumptions as to the complexity of the phenomena they deal with.

The operational approach not only spares Jensen the task of trying to understand the nature of intelligence, it also enables him to draw an extremely powerful conclusion from statistical analyses of I.Q. test scores:—

> Regardless of what it is that our tests measure, the heritability tells us how much of the variance in these measurements is due to genetic factors.

Because this assertion holds the key to Jensen's entire argument, we shall analyze it in some detail.

HERITABILITY

In the statement just quoted, Jensen uses the term *heritability* in a specific technical sense that must be elucidated before the statement can be analyzed. Suppose that we have measured an individual character like height or weight within a given population. The two most fundamental statistical properties of a character are its *mean* and its *variance*. The mean is the average of the measurements; the variance is the average of the squared differences between the individual measurements and the mean. The variance is the most convenient single measure of the spread of individual measurements within a population. Now, this spread results partly from genetic and partly from non-genetic causes. *But this does not mean, nor is it true in*

124

general, that a definite fraction of the spread, as measured by the variance, can be attributed to genetic factors and the rest to non-genetic factors. The variance splits up into separate genetic and non-genetic parts only if each measurement can be expressed as the sum of *statistically independent* genetic and non-genetic contributions—that is, only if the relevant genetic and non-genetic factors contribute additively and independently to the character in question. (A criterion for statistical independence will be given later.) In this case the genetic fraction or percentage of the variance is called the heritability.

Characters like eye color and blood type, which are entirely genetically determined, have heritability 1. In general, however, the heritability of a character depends on the population considered and on the range of relevant non-genetic factors. Reducing this range always increases the heritability because it increases the relative importance of the genetic contribution to the variance.

It is not easy to find realistic examples of metric characters affected independently by genetic and non-genetic factors. Human height is a possible, though not a proven, example, provided we restrict ourselves to ethnically homogeneous populations. Giraffe height, on the other hand, is a counterexample, since a giraffe's nutritional opportunities may depend strongly on his genetic endowment. Human weight is another counterexample: on a given diet one person may gain weight while another loses weight.

Let us suppose, however, that we have reason to believe that a given character is in fact the sum of independent genetic and environmental contributions. To calculate its heritability we need to be able to estimate either the genetic or the environmental contribution to its variance. This can be done if, for example, the population contains a large number of split pairs of one-egg twins. By a split pair I mean one whose members have been separated since birth and reared in randomly selected, statistically uncorrelated environments. All observable differences between such twins are environmental in origin, and the environmental differences are, by assumption, representative

125

of those between individuals selected at random from the reference population. If, in addition, the genotypes of the twins are representative of those in the population as a whole, then, using elementary statistical techniques, one can derive separate estimates for the genetic and environmental contributions to the variance of any metric character that satisfies the assumptions of additivity and independence. The same calculations serve to check these assumptions.

If a suitably representative population of split twin-pairs is not available, one can carry out a similar but slightly more complicated analysis using pairs of genetically related individuals. In this case, however, one needs to know what degree of statistical correlation between the genetic contributions to a given character results from a given degree of genetic relationship. This information is available only for relatively simple characters such as those studied by Mendel in his classic experiments. For most characters of interest to students of animal genetics, the necessary information must be supplied by admittedly oversimplified theoretical considerations. Where human characters are concerned, the fact that mating patterns are both uncontrolled and non-random introduces a further source of uncertainty into the calculation.

Although geneticists can often carry out carefully controlled experiments involving known variations in genetic and environmental factors, the lack of reliable theoretical information concerning the genetic basis of complex characters makes the concept of heritability less useful than one might at first sight suppose. In poultry, for example, the heritabilities of such economically important characters as adult body weight, egg weight, shell thickness, etc., have been repeatedly estimated. Yet for most such characters the estimates span a considerable range—sometimes as great as 50% (Lerner, 1968). Again, estimates of milk yield in dairy cattle range from 25% to 90%. This spread does not result from random errors in individual estimates but from the fact that different methods, which in theory ought to be equivalent, yield systematically different heritability estimates. As Waddington (1957) has remarked in a similar context,

"The statistical techniques available [for the analysis of heritability], although imposing and indeed intimidating to most biologists, are in fact very weak and unhandy tools."

The assumption that genetic and environmental factors contribute additively and independently to a phenotypic character is, on general grounds, highly suspect. From a purely mathematical point of view, additivity is an exceedingly special property. Moreover, a character that happens to have this property when measured on one scale would lose it under a nonlinear transformation to a different scale of measurement. Additivity is therefore a plausible postulate only when there exists some specific biological justification for it. For complex animal characters there is little reason to expect additivity and independence to prevail. On the contrary, such characters usually reflect a complicated developmental process in which genetic and environmental factors are inextricably mingled.

It is easy enough to produce more general mathematical models in which genetic and environmental factors contribute nonadditively and nonindependently to the expression of a character. The difficulty with such models is that they are too flexible to be useful. The available statistical data do not suffice to evaluate the parameters needed to specify the model. Thus in the absence of a deeper understanding of the genetic and developmental factors affecting complex animal characters, the theory of heritability must operate within a severely restricted range.

I.Q. AS A MEASURE OF INTELLIGENCE

We are now ready to analyze the key assertion quoted earlier:—"Regardless of what it is that our tests measure, the heritability tells us how much of the variance of these measurements is due to genetic factors." Implicit in this statement are two distinct assumptions: that I.Q. is a phenotypic character having the mathematical structure (additivity and independence of the genetic and environmental contributions) presupposed by the theory of heritability; and that—assuming this condition to be fulfilled—the heritability of I.Q. can be estimated from

127

existing data. Now, the I.Q. data that Jensen and others have analyzed were gathered in eight countries and four continents, over a period of 50 years, by investigators using a wide variety of mental tests and testing procedures. Geneticists and other natural scientists who make conventional scientific measurements under controlled conditions know from bitter experience how wayward and recalcitrant, how insensitive to the needs and wishes of theoreticians, such measurements can be. Their experience hardly leads one to anticipate that the results of mental tests constructed in accordance with unformulated, subjective and largely arbitrary criteria possess the special mathematical structure needed to define heritability. It is difficult to imagine how this happy result could have been achieved except through the operation of collective serendipity on a scale unprecedented in the annals of science. Nevertheless, let us examine the case on its merits.

At the very outset we have to ask: Is I.Q. a valid measure of intelligence? Jensen and Herrnstein assure us that it is. "The most important fact about intelligence is that we can measure it," says Jensen, while Herrnstein remarks that the "objective measurement of intelligence" is psychology's "most telling accomplishment." I find these claims difficult to understand. To begin with, the "objective measurement" does not belong to the same *logical category* as what it purports to measure. I.Q. does not measure an individual phenotypic character like height or weight; it is a measure of the rank order or relative standing of test scores in a given population. Thus the statement, "A has an I.Q. of 100" means that half the members of a certain reference population scored lower than A on a certain set of tests and half scored higher. "B has an I.Q. of 115" means that 68% of the reference population scored lower than B and 32% higher, and so on. (I.Q. tests are so constructed that the frequency distribution of test scores in the reference population conforms as closely as possible to a normal distribution—the familiar bell-shaped curve—centered on the value of 100 and having a half-width or standard deviation [the square root of the variance] of 15 points.) To call I.Q. a measure of intelligence conforms neither to ordinary educated usage nor to elementary logic.

One might perhaps be tempted to dismiss this objection as a mere logical quibble. If I.Q. itself belongs to the wrong logical category to be a measure of intelligence, why not use actual test scores? One difficulty with this proposal is the multiplicity and diversity of mental tests, all with equally valid claims. (This is part of the price that must be paid for a strictly "operational" definition of intelligence.) Even if one were to decide quite arbitrarily to subscribe to a particular brand of mental test, one would still need to administer different versions of it to different age groups. An appearance of uniformity is secured only by forcing the results of each test to fit the same Procrustean bed (the normal distribution). But this mathematical operation cannot convert an index of rank order on tests having an unspecified and largely arbitrary content into an "objective measure of intelligence." Even Burt (1956), a convinced hereditarian whose work forms the mainstay of Jensen's technical argument, recognized this difficulty. "Differences in this hypothetical ability [intelligence]," he wrote, "*cannot* be directly measured. We can, however, systematically observe relevant aspects of the child's behavior and record his performances on standardized tests; and in this way we can usually arrive at a reasonably reliable and valid estimate of his 'intelligence' in the sense defined." (Emphasis added. Earlier in the paper cited above, Burt defines intelligence as "an innate, general, cognitive factor.") Burt's conviction that intelligence cannot be directly or objectively measured—a conviction bred by over half a century of active observation—profoundly influenced his practical approach to the problem. In assessing children's intelligence, Burt and his assistants used group tests, but also relied heavily on the subjective impressions of teachers. When a discrepancy arose between a teacher's assessment and the results of group tests, the child was retested individually, if necessary more than once. Burt's final assessments may be "reliable and valid," as he claims, but they are certainly not objective, nor did he consider them to be so.

129

The fact that I.Q. cannot, for purely logical reasons, be an objective measure of intelligence (or of any other individual characteristic) does not automatically invalidate Jensen's arguments concerning heritability. Rank order on a mental test could still be, as Burt suggested, an *indirect* measure of intelligence. To illustrate this point, suppose that members of a superintelligent race of octopuses, unable to construct rigid measuring rods but versed in statistical techniques, wished to measure tentacle length. Through appropriate tests of performance they might be able to establish rank order of tentacle length in individual age groups. By forcing the frequency distribution of rank order in each group to fit a normal distribution with mean 100 and standard deviation 15, they would arrive at a T.Q. (tentacle quotient) for each octopus. In all probability, differences in T.Q. would turn out to be closely proportional to differences in actual tentacle length within a given age group, though the factor of proportionality would vary in an unknown way from one group to another. Thus our hypothetical race of octopuses would be able to *infer* relative tentacle length within an age group from information about rank order. This inference evidently hinges on the assumption that tentacle length, which the octopuses cannot measure directly, is in reality normally distributed within each age group.

SOME TACIT ASSUMPTIONS UNMASKED AND ANALYZED

Similarly, the *inference* that I.Q. is a measure of intelligence depends on certain assumptions, namely: (a) that there exists an underlying one-dimensional, metric character related to I.Q. in a one-to-one way, as tentacle length is related to T.Q., and (b) that the values assumed by this character in a suitable reference population are normally distributed.

If these assumptions do not in themselves constitute a theory of human intelligence, they severely restrict the range of possible theories. Once again we see that the "operational stance," though motivated by a laudable desire to avoid theoretical judgments, cannot in fact dispense with them. The choice between a theoretical approach and an empirical one is illusory; we can only choose between explicit theory and implicit theory. But let us examine the assumptions on their own merits.

The first assumption is pure metaphysics. Assertions about the existence of unobservable properties cannot be proved or disproved; their acceptance demands an act of faith. Let us perform this act, however—at least provisionally—so that we can examine the second assumption, which asserts that the underlying metric character postulated in the first assumption is normally distributed in suitably chosen reference populations. Why normally distributed? A possible answer to this question is suggested by a remark quoted by the great French mathematician Henri Poincaré: "Everybody believes in the [normal distribution]: the experimenters because they think it can be proved by mathematics, the mathematicians because it has been established by observation." Nowadays both experimenters and mathematicians know better. Generally speaking, we should expect to find a normal frequency distribution when the variable part of the measurements in question can be expressed as the sum of many individually small, mutually independent, variable contributions. This is thought to be the case for a number of metric characters of animals such as birth weight in cattle, staple length of wool, and (perhaps) tentacle length in octopuses. It is not the case, on the other hand, for measurements of most kinds of skill or proficiency. Golf scores, for example, are not likely to be normally distributed because proficiency in golf does not result from the combined action of a large number of individually small and mutually independent factors.

What about mental ability? Jensen and Herrnstein believe that insight into its nature can be gained by studying the ways in which people have tried to measure it. Jensen argues that because different mental tests agree moderately well among themselves, they must be probing a common factor (Spearman's *g*). Some tests, say Jensen, are "heavily loaded with *g*," others not so heavily loaded. Thus *g* is something like the pork in cans labelled "pork and beans."

Herrnstein takes a less metaphysical line. Since intelligence is what intelligence tests measure, he argues, what needs to be decided is what we *want* intelligence tests to measure. This is to be decided by "subjective judgment" based on "common expectations" as to the "instrument." "In the case of intelligence, common expectations center around the common purposes of intelligence testing—predicting success in school, suitability for various occupations, intellectual achievement in life." Thus Herrnstein defines intelligence "instrumentally" as the attribute that successfully predicts success in enterprises whose success is commonly believed to depend strongly on . . . intelligence. That is, intelligence is what is measured by tests that successfully predict success in enterprises whose success is commonly believed to depend strongly on what is measured by tests that successfully predict success in enterprises whose success is commonly believed to depend strongly on. . . .

Whatever the philosophical merits of the definitions offered by Jensen and Herrnstein, they offer little insight into the question at hand: does intelligence depend on genetic and environmental factors in the manner required by heritability theory? In other words, is the heritability of intelligence a meaningful concept? To pursue this question we must go outside the theoretical framework of Jensen's discussion.

INTELLIGENCE DEFINED; COGNITIVE DEVELOPMENT

Many modern workers believe that intelligence can usefully be defined as information-processing ability. As a physical scientist, I find this definition irresistible. To begin with, it permits us to distinguish as many qualitatively different kinds of information as we may find it useful to do. Moreover, because information is a precisely defined mathematical concept, there is no obvious reason why it should not be possible to devise practical methods for reliably measuring the ability to process it. (In its broadest sense information-processing involves problem-solving as well as the extraction and rearrangement of data.) Whether or not such tests would be accurate predictors of "success" I do not know. They could, however, be usefully employed in assessing the effectiveness of teachers, educational procedures and curricula.

Information-processing skills, like other skills, are not innate, but develop over the course of time. What is the nature of this development? Consider such complex skills as skiing or playing the piano. In order to acquire an advanced technique one must acquire in succession a number of intermediate techniques. Each of these enables one to perform competently at a certain level of difficulty, and each must be thoroughly mastered before one can pass to the next level. The passage to a higher level always involves the mastery of qualitatively new techniques. Through systematic observations carried out over half a century with the help of numerous collaborators, Jean Piaget (1952) has demonstrated that basic cognitive structures also develop in this way, and he has traced the development of a great many of these structures in meticulous detail. Each new structure is always more highly organized and more differentiated than its predecessor. At the same time it is more adequate to a specific environmental challenge. The intermediate stages in the development of a given structure are not rigidly predetermined (there are many different ways of learning to read or ski or play the piano), nor is the rate at which an individual passes through them, but in every case cognitive development follows two basic rules (Piaget 1967): "Every genesis emanates from a structure and culminates in another structure. Conversely, every structure has a genesis."

Cognitive development may be compared to the building of a house. Logic and the laws of physics demand that the various stages be completed in a definite order: the foundations before the frame, the frame before the walls, the walls before the roof. The finished product will depend no doubt on the skill of the builder and on the available materials, but it will also depend on the builder's intentions and on the nature of the environmental challenge. Similarly, although cognitive development is undoubtedly strongly influenced by genetic factors, it represents an adaptation of the human organism to its environment and

133

must therefore be strongly influenced by the nature of the environmental challenge. Thus we may expect cultural factors to play an important part in shaping all the higher cognitive skills, for the environmental challenges that are relevant to these skills are largely determined by cultural context.

GENETIC-ENVIRONMENTAL INTERACTION

If intelligence, or at least its potentially measurable aspects, can be identified with information-processing skills and if the preceding very rough account of how these skills develop is substantially correct, then it seems highly unlikely that scores achieved on mental tests can have the mathematical properties that we have been discussing—properties needed to make "heritability of I.Q." a meaningful concept. The information-processing skills assessed by mental tests result from developmental processes in which genetic and non-genetic factors interact continuously. The more relevant a given task is to an individual's specific environmental challenges, the more important are the effects of this interaction. Thus a child growing up in circumstances that provide motivation, reward and opportunity for the acquisition of verbal skills will achieve a higher level of verbal proficiency than his twin reared in an environment hostile to this kind of development. Even if two genetically unlike individuals grow up in the same circumstances—for example, two-egg twins reared together—we cannot assume (as Jensen, Herrnstein and other hereditarians usually do) that the relevant non-genetic factors are the same for both. If one twin has greater verbal aptitude or is more strongly motivated to acquire verbal skills (usually the two factors go together), he will devote more time and effort to this kind of learning than his twin. Thus differences between scores on tests of verbal proficiency will not reflect genetic differences only, but also—perhaps predominantly—differences between the ways in which the genetic endowments of the twins have interacted with their common environment.

134

One might be tempted to classify these interactive contributions to developed skills as genetic, on the grounds that they are not purely environmental and that the genetic factor in the interaction plays the active role. In technical discussions, however, common sense must accomodate itself to definitions and conventions laid down at the outset. If we redraw the line that separates genetic and non-genetic factors we must formulate a new theory of inheritance; if we wish to use the existing theory we must stick to the definitions that it presupposes.

DOES THE I.Q. DATA FIT THE THEORY OF HERITABILITY?

Up till now we have concerned ourselves with the first of the two implicit assumptions underlying Jensen's key assertion about the interpretation of heritability estimates, namely, the assumption that intelligence is a phenotypic character to which the theory of heritability can be applied. We have found no plausible grounds for supposing that genetic and environmental factors contribute to the development of intelligence in the simple way required by heritability theory. To this objection Jensen and Herrnstein might reply as follows:—"Discussions of 'meaning,' 'mathematical structure' and 'logical categories' are irrelevant. I.Q. test scores and the statistical quantities that can be derived from them (means, variances and correlations) are hard data. There is nothing to prevent us from applying heritability theory to this data and seeing whether or not it fits. If the theory does fit, we may reasonably assume that it applies to this data, whatever its provenance."

This argument has some validity. If the heritability theory *did* apply to I.Q. test scores and the statistics derived from them, these statistics would simultaneously satisfy a large number of numerical relations, like the steel girders composing a complex rigid structure. Conversely, if all these relations were indeed accurately satisfied by the statistical data, we would have good reason to suppose that the theory applied to them in spite of *a priori* arguments to the contrary. Yet such arguments do serve an important purpose: they help us to decide how good

135

the evidence must be to convince us that the theory really does fit the data. Suppose that an astronomer, having made several observations of a newly discovered planet, tries to determine its orbit using Newton's theory of gravitation. If he applies the theory correctly, he can be virtually certain that any discrepancy between the theory and his observations results from observational error: previous experience has firmly established Newton's theory and its applicability to the motion of planets. When the validity or applicability of a theory is not so well established, however, it may not be easy to decide how much of the discrepancy between theory and observation to attribute to experimental error and how much to error or incompleteness in the theoretical description. In such cases a competent scientist bases his judgment on all the relevant theoretical and observational information available to him. If that information strongly suggests that a given theory does not apply to given data, he will demand highly convincing evidence of internal consistency before taking seriously claims based on a theoretical analysis of the data.

The data that Jensen, Burt and other hereditarians have analyzed consists mainly of *correlations* between the measured I.Q.'s of more or less closely related persons living in more or less similar environments. (Correlation is a measure of similarity between the *rank orders* of two measurements. The statement "height and weight are positively correlated" means that taller subjects *tend to be* heavier.) Such data has usually shown that the I.Q.'s of more closely related people tend to be more highly correlated than those between less closely related people; also that the I.Q.'s of children growing up in similar circumstances tend to be more highly correlated than those of children growing up in dissimilar circumstances. For pairs of children reared together, the measured correlations increase systematically with increasing genetic similarity. Thus the I.Q.'s of one-egg (identical) twins tend to be more highly correlated than those of two-egg (fraternal) twins, which in turn tend to be more highly correlated than the I.Q.'s of unrelated children reared together. These findings show that I.Q. is strongly influenced by both genetic and environmental factors. Can we disentangle these factors? "By evaluating the total evidence," writes Herrnstein, "and by a procedure too technical to explain here, Jensen concluded (as have most of the other experts in the field) that the genetic factor is worth about 80% and that only 20% is left to everything else . . ."

As summarized by Herrnstein, the evidence on which this conclusion rests seems quite impressive. Herrnstein compares the "actual" values of I.Q. correlations between relatives with "theoretical" correlations calculated on the assumption that non-genetic effects on I.Q. are negligible. In every case the agreement seems to be very close:—

Uncle's (or aunt's) I.Q. should, by the genes alone, correlate with nephew's (or niece's) by a value of 31%; the actual value is 34%. The correlation between grandparent and grandchild should, on genetic grounds alone, also be 31%, whereas the actual correlation is 27%, again a small discrepancy. And finally for this brief survey, the predicted correlation between parent and child, by genes alone, is 49%, whereas the actual correlation is 50% using the parents' adult I.Q. and 56% using the parents' childhood I.Q.'s—in either case too small a difference to quibble about.

But let us take a closer look. What does Herrnstein mean by the word "actual" in the passage just quoted? "The foregoing figures," he writes, "are lifted directly out of Jensen's famous article, figures that he himself culled from the literature on intelligence testing." Referring to Jensen's article, we do indeed find the figures quoted by Herrnstein, in a column headed "obtained median correlation." How is the "median" correlation related to the "actual" correlation? Can we assert that the actual value of a quantity lies close to the median of several measurements of that quantity? As every working scientist knows, the answer to this question is, No, not in general. All that can be said is that, in the absence of systematic errors, the actual value is likely to lie within a range of values comparable to the range spanned by the actual measurements (if there are enough of them).

What ranges do the I.Q. correlations span? Jensen's paper does not supply this important information. His table, however, is adapted from one given by Burt, who, in order to compare his own correlation measurements with those of previous investigators, tabulated the medians of correlation measurements collected by Erlenmeyer-Kimling and Jarvik (1964). Burt did not display the actual ranges of the measured correlations, but he did mention that several of them were large and gave one example: for siblings reared together, the correlations obtained in 55 studies range from .3 to .8 and are spread almost uniformly over the entire range. The correlations reported between parent and child in 11 studies—to give a second example—range from about .2 to about .8.

But these figures still do not tell the whole story. What do the reported correlations actually mean? Each reported correlation refers to a particular sample and to a particular test or set of tests. How homogeneous are the samples with respect to non-genetic variables? How meaningful is it to combine correlations referring to population samples and tests differing in unspecified and unknown ways? The answers to these hard but important questions are to be found, if they are to be found at all, in the primary sources. As we move farther and farther away from these sources, the errors and uncertainties in the data become less and less noticeable, until at last, in the pages of *The Atlantic Monthly*, only the "actual values" remain. Like the reputations of saints, scientific data often improve with transmission.

The "theoretical correlations" quoted by Herrnstein have undergone a similar transformation. The theory in question is not the one usually applied by geneticists to estimate the heritability of polygenic characteristics, but a modified version of that theory especially devised by Burt and Howard (1956) to improve the agreement with their correlation data—data based, incidentally, on Burt's semi-objective assessments of intelligence.

What, then, can we infer from the data on I.Q. correlations? If genetic factors did not appreciably influence I.Q., we would expect to find no appreciable differences between the I.Q. correlations of one-egg twins, two-egg twins and unrelated children reared in the same home. In fact, the measured correlations tend to be greater for one-egg twins and siblings than for unrelated children reared in the same home—although the ranges overlap considerably. This indicates that genetic factors undoubtedly do influence I.Q. significantly—but not necessarily in the manner presupposed by the heritability theory. The internal consistency of the reported data is far too low to lend credence to claims that I.Q. measurements have the mathematical structure required by that theory.

I.Q. AND CULTURE

This brings us to the important question of how cultural factors affect I.Q. correlations. Jensen's views on this question are instructive. He asserts that only genetic factors can *raise* heritability estimates, and that cultural bias in a test always *lowers* the heritability of the results. In discussing these assertions we can avoid unnecessary confusion by regarding "heritability estimates" as purely formal mathematical quantities defined in terms of measured correlations. One such "heritability estimate," for example, is provided by the I.Q. correlation between one-egg twins reared separately, another is given by twice the difference between the I.Q. correlations of one-egg and two-egg twins, and so on. As we have seen, different "estimates" of this kind do not agree among themselves, and none of them can be interpreted as measuring the genetic fraction of I.Q. variance in a given population.

Do cultural factors systematically affect performance on I.Q. tests? Hereditarians usually argue that such effects are probably small, because the skills assessed by I.Q. tests are not systematically taught in school. Hence, they argue, all children have the same opportunity to learn them. It is (unfortunately) true that many of these skills are not taught effectively in schools, but no one who has actually visited classrooms in suburban and in ghetto schools would deny that they are usually taught more effectively in the former than in the latter. Moreover, they are deliberately and effectively taught in homes where learning is valued for its own sake. Children who grow up in such homes learn to speak grammatically, to use words with precision, to get information and entertainment from books, to argue consequentially, to solve abstract problems, and to set a high value on these and similar activities. Such home environments tend strongly to run in families and to occur more frequently in some ethnic groups than in others.

In her classic study of some leading American scientists, Anne Roe (1952) discovered that an unexpectedly large proportion of her subjects were the sons of professional men. She suggested as the most likely explanation for this finding the fact that her subjects grew up in homes where

> for one reason or another learning was valued for its own sake. The social and economic advantages associated with it were not scorned, but they were not the important factor. The interest of many of these men took an intellectual form at quite an early age. This would not be possible if they were not in contact of some sort with such interests and if these did not have value for them. This can be true even in homes where it is not taken for granted that the sons will go to college.

We do not choose our cultural background but are born into it. For this reason people related by blood are more likely to share a common cultural background and common cultural values than unrelated persons. Since parental values help to shape children's intellectual development, it is clear that cultural factors affect I.Q. correlations between relatives in roughly the same way as genetic factors. The correspondence between cultural and genetic effects is not, of course, perfect. For example, if cultural factors alone were important, we would expect to find nearly the same correlations between the test scores of one-egg and two-egg twins (which is what Scarr-Salapatek (1971b) actually has found in a recent study of Philadelphia school children). On the other hand, heritability estimates based on I.Q. correlations between separated one-egg twins would probably be quite high, because in those cases where the separated twins are not actually reared by relatives, adoption agencies usually strive to match the cultural backgrounds of natural and adoptive parents. In short, cultural factors may be expected to increase some heritability estimates and to decrease others. The available observational evidence is at least consistent with the hypothesis that cultural factors contribute heavily to measured I.Q. correlations.

Culture is, of course, not the only mock-genetic environmental factor that systematically influences I.Q. Because cultural values, wealth, social status, occupational and educational levels are all more or less strongly correlated with one another as well as with I.Q., and because they are all transmitted from generation to generation in roughly the same way as genetic information, it would obviously be very difficult under the best of circumstances to disentangle the genetic factors affecting I.Q. from the non-genetic factors. We have seen, however, that even if all these systematic non-genetic factors were absent, such a separation could not be accomplished through the application of heritability theory, because I.Q. measurements do not satisfy that theory's requirements.

Jensen and other hereditarians not only fail to take cultural and other environmental factors adequately into account, they also ignore *genetic but non-cognitive* factors which interact in complex and as yet little understood ways with each other, with cognitive factors and with the environment. Among such factors are sex, color, temperament and physical appearance. Thus in societies where mathematical ability is considered unfeminine and femininity is prized, women tend not to develop mathematical ability. Again, skepticism and curiosity may help a middle-class child to develop scientific ability but only cause trouble for a ghetto child. And in societies like our own, where selection and advancement mechanisms often employ positive feedback (nothing succeeds like success), small "initial" differences in genetic or environmental endowment often get greatly amplified. This is another way of saying that genetic-environmental interaction may well dominate the development of the skills that I.Q. tests assess.

So far we have been chiefly concerned with the arguments by which Jensen and other hereditarians have sought to establish the high heritability of I.Q. We have seen that these arguments do not hold water. In the first place, the "heritability of I.Q." is a pseudo-concept like "the sexuality of fractions" or "the analyticity of the ocean." Assigning a numerical value to the "heritability of I.Q." does not, of course, make the concept more meaningful, any more than assigning a numerical value to the sexuality of fractions would make *that* concept more meaningful. In the second place, even if we had a theory of inheritance that could be applied to I.Q. test scores, we could not apply it to the correlation data employed by Jensen. A scientific theory, like a racing car, needs the right grade of fuel. Jensen's data are to scientific data as unrefined petroleum is to high-test gasoline. Jensen and Herrnstein would have us believe that we can gain important insights into human intelligence and its inheritance by subjecting measurements that we do not understand to a mathematical analysis that we cannot justify. Unfortunately, many people appear to be susceptible to such beliefs, which have their roots in a widespread tendency to attribute magical efficacy to mathematics in almost any context. The perennial popularity of astrology is probably an expression of this tendency. Astrology is based, after all, on hard numerical data, and the success and internal consistency of its predictions are customarily offered as evidence for its validity. The most important difference between astrology and the Jensen-Herrnstein brand of intellectual Calvinism is not methodological but philosophical; one school believes that man's fate is written in the stars, the other that it runs in his genes.

Jensen's and Herrnstein's central thesis is that certain cognitive skills—those involving abstract reasoning and problem solving—cannot be taught effectively to children with low I.Q.'s. From this thesis, and from it alone, flow all the disturbing educational, social and political inferences drawn by these authors. If social and educational reforms could raise the general level of mental abilities to the point where people with I.Q.'s of 85 were able to solve calculus problems and read French, rank order on mental tests would no longer seem very important. It is precisely this possibility that Jensen's argument seeks to rule out. For, if only a small fraction of the difference in average I.Q. between children living in Scarsdale and in Bedford-Stuyvesant can be attributed to environmental differences, it seems unrealistic to expect environmental improvements to bring about substantial increases in the general level of intelligence.

Now, even if Jensen's theoretical considerations and his analysis of data were beyond reproach, they would afford a singularly indirect means of testing his key thesis. The question to be answered is whether appropriate forms of intervention can substantially raise (a) the rate at which children acquire the abilities tested by I.Q. tests and/or (b) final levels of achievement. This question can be answered experimentally, and it has been. Since we do not yet know precisely what forms of intervention are most effective for different children, negative results (such as the alleged failure of compensatory education) carry little weight. On the other hand, all positive results are relevant. For if I.Q. can be substantially and consistently raised—by no matter what means—it obviously cannot reflect a fixed mental capacity.

The professional literature abounds in reports of studies that have achieved striking positive results. Several of these are cited by Scarr-Salapatek (1971a) in a critical review of recent hereditarian literature. In one extended study,

> the Milwaukee Project, in which subjects are ghetto children whose mothers' I.Q.'s are less than 70, intervention began soon after the children were born. Over a four-year period Heber has intensively tutored the children for several hours every day and has produced an enormous I.Q. difference between the experimental group (mean I.Q. 127) and a control group (mean I.Q. 90).

Has intensive tutoring engendered in these ghetto children a previously absent "capacity" for abstract reasoning and problem solving?

In a study published in 1949 and frequently cited in the psychological literature, Skodak and Skeels compared the I.Q.'s of adopted children in a certain sample with those of their biological mothers, whose environments were systematically poorer than those of the adoptive mothers. They found a 20 point mean difference in favor of the children, although the rank order of the children's I.Q.'s closely resembled that of their biological mothers.

Many tests have shown that blacks living in the urban north score systematically higher on I.Q. tests than those living in the rural south. For many years hereditarians and environmentalists debated the interpretation of this finding. The environmentalists attributed the systematic I.Q. difference to environmental differences, the hereditarians to selective migration (they argued that the migrants could be expected to be more energetic and intelligent than the stay-at-homes). The environmental interpretation was decisively vindicated in 1935 by O. Klineberg, who showed that the I.Q.'s of migrant children increased systematically and substantially with length of residence in the north. In New York (in the early 1930's) migrant black children with 8 years of schooling had approximately the same average I.Q. as whites. These important findings were fully confirmed by E. S. Lee (1951), who, 15 years later, repeated Klineberg's experiment in Philadelphia. Additional studies bearing on I.Q. differences between ethnic groups are reviewed and analyzed by L. Plotkin (1971).

Teachers and therapists who work with children suffering neuropsychiatric disorders (including emotional and perceptual disturbances) regularly report large increases in their tested I.Q.'s. One remedial reading teacher of my acquaintance works exclusively with "ineducable" children. So far she has not had a single failure; every one of her pupils has learned to read. And reading, of course, provides the indispensable basis for acquiring most of the higher cognitive skills.

THE HYPOTHESIS OF UNLIMITED EDUCABILITY

That the growth of intelligence is controlled in part by genetic factors seems beyond doubt. The significant questions are, "What are these factors?" "How do they operate?" "How do they inter-

144

act with non-cognitive and environmental factors?" Experience suggests that children differ in the ease with which they acquire specific kinds of cognitive skills as well as in the intensity of their cognitive drives or appetites. But cognitive appetites, like other appetites, can be whetted or dulled. Nor are aptitude and appetite the only relevant factors. Everyone can cite case histories in which motivation has more than compensated for a deficit in aptitude. There are excellent skiers, violinists and scientists who have little natural aptitude for any of these activities. None of them will win international acclaim, but few of them will mind. I know of no theoretical or experimental evidence to contradict the assumption that everyone in the normal range of intelligence could, if sufficiently motivated, and given sufficient time, acquire the basic cognitive abilities demanded by such professions as law, medicine and business administration.

Once we stop thinking of human intelligence as static and predetermined, and instead focus our attention on the growth of cognitive skills and on how the interaction between cognitive, non-cognitive and environmental factors affects this growth, the systematic differences in test performance between ethnic groups appear in a new light. Because cognitive development is a cumulative process, it is strongly influenced by small systematic effects acting over an extended period. Information-processing ability grows roughly in the same way as money in a savings account: the rate of growth is proportional to the accumulated capital. Hence a small increase or decrease in the interest rate will ultimately make a very large difference in the amount accumulated. Now, the "cognitive interest rate" reflects genetic, cultural and social factors, all interacting in a complicated way. Membership in the Afro-American ethnic group is a social factor (based in part on noncognitive genetic factors) that, in the prevailing social context, contributes negatively to the cognitive interest rate. The amount of the negative contribution varies from person to person, being generally greatest for the most disadvantaged. But there is no doubt that it is always present to some extent. In these circumstances we should expect to find exactly the kind of group differences that we do find. I think it is important to take note of these differences. They are valuable indices of our society's persistent failure to eradicate the blight of racism.

It may be that the assumption of unlimited educability will one day be shown to be false. But until then, it could usefully be adopted as a working hypothesis by educators, social scientists and politicians. We have seen that the widely held belief in fixed mental capacity as measured by I.Q. has no valid scientific basis. As a device for predicting scholastic success (and thereby for helping to form the expectations of teachers, parents and students), as a criterion for deciding that certain children should be excluded from certain kinds of education, and as a lever for shifting the burden of scholastic failure from schools and teachers to students, the I.Q. test has indeed been, in Herrnstein's words, "a potent instrument"—potent and exceedingly mischievous.

Admirers of I.Q. tests usually lay great stress on their predictive power. They marvel that a one-hour test administered to a child at the age of eight can predict with considerable accuracy whether he will finish college. But, as Burt and his associates have clearly demonstrated, teachers' subjective assessments afford even more reliable predictors. This is almost a truism. If scholastic success is to be predictable, it must be reasonably consistent at different age levels (otherwise there is nothing to predict). But if it is consistent, then it is its own best predictor. Johnny's second-grade teacher can do at least as well as the man from ETS. This does not mean that mental tests are useless. On the contrary, sound methods for measuring information-processing ability and the growth of specific cognitive skills could be extremely useful to psychologists and educators—not as instruments for predicting scholastic success but as tools for studying how children learn and as standards for assessing the effectiveness of teaching methods.

CONCLUSIONS

To what extent are differences in human intelligence caused by differences in environment, and to what extent by differences

146

in genetic endowment? Are there systematic differences in native intelligence between races or ethnic groups? Jensen, Herrnstein, Eysenck, Shockley and others assure us that these questions are legitimate subjects for scientific investigation; that intelligence tests and statistical analyses of test results have already gone a long way toward answering them; that the same techniques can be used to reduce still further the remaining uncertainties; that the results so far obtained clearly establish that differences in genetic endowment are chiefly responsible for differences in performance on intelligence tests; that reported differences in mean I.Q. between Afro- and European-Americans may well be genetically based; and that educational, social and political policy decisions should take these "scientific findings" into account. We have seen, however, that the arguments put forward to support these claims are unsound. I.Q. scores and correlations are not measurements in any sense known to the natural sciences, and "heritability estimates" based on them have as much scientific validity as horoscopes. Perhaps the single most important fact about human intelligence is its enormous and as yet ungauged capacity for growth and adaptation. The more insight we gain into cognitive development, the less meaningful seems any attempt to isolate and measure differences in genetic endowment—and the less important. In every natural science there are certain questions that can profitably be asked at a given stage in the development of that science, and certain questions that cannot. Chemistry and astronomy grew out of attempts to answer the questions, How can base metals be transmuted into gold? How do the heavenly bodies control human destiny? Chemistry and astronomy never answered these questions, they outgrew them. Similarly, the development of psychology during the present century has made the questions posed at the beginning of this paragraph seem increasingly sterile and artificial. Why, then, are they now being revived?

Earlier in this article I suggested that a combination of cultural, historical and political factors tempts us to seek easy "scientific" solutions to hard social problems. But this explanation is incomplete. It leaves out a crucial psychological factor: once we have acquired a skill we find it hard to believe that it was not always "there," a latent image waiting to be developed by time and experience. The complex muscular responses of an expert skier to a difficult trail are, to him, as instinctive as a baby's reaction to an unexpected loud noise. For this reason the doctrine of innate mental capacity exercises an intuitive appeal that developmental accounts can never quite match. This, however, makes it all the more important to scrutinize critically the logical, methodological and psychological underpinnings of that doctrine.

REFERENCES

Burt, C., The Genetic Determination of Differences in Intelligence: A Study of Monozygotic Twins Reared Together and Apart. British Journal of Psychology, 1966, 57, 1 and 2, 137–153.

Burt, C. and Howard, M., The Multifactorial Theory of Inheritance and its Application to Intelligence. *British Journal of Statistical Psychology*, 1956, *9*, 95–131.

Erlenmeyer-Kimling, L. and Jarvik, L. F., Genetics and Intelligence. *Science*, 1964, *142*, 1477–1479.

Eysenck, H. J., The I.Q. Argument, Race, Intelligence and Education. New York: The Library Press, 1971.

Fehr, F. S., Critique of Hereditarian Accounts. *Harvard Educational Review*, 1969, *39*, 571–580.

Herrnstein, R. J., I.Q. *The Atlantic Monthly*, 1971, *228*, 43–64.

Jensen, A. R., How Much Can We Boost I.Q. and Scholastic Achievement? *Harvard Educational Review*, 1969, *39*.

Klineberg, O., *Negro Intelligence and Selective Migration.* New York: Columbia University Press, 1935.

Lee, E. S., Negro Intelligence and Selective Migration: A Philadelphia Test of the Klineberg Hypothesis. *American Sociological Review*, 1951, *16*.

Lerner, I. M., *Heredity, Evolution and Society*, San Francisco: W. H. Freeman and Company, 1968.

Lewontin, R. C., Race and Intelligence. *Bulletin of the Atomic Scientists*, March 1970, *2–8*.

Piaget, J., *The Origins of Intelligence in Children*. New York: International Universities Press, 1952.

———, *Six Psychological Studies*. New York: Random House, 1967.

Plotkin, L., Negro Intelligence and the Jensen Hypothesis. *The New York Statistician*, 1971, *22*, 3–7.

Roe, Anne, *The Making of a Scientist*. New York: Dodd, Mead, and Company, 1953.

Scarr-Salapatek, S., Unknowns in the I.Q. Equation. *Science*, 1971, *174*, 1223–1228.

———, Race, Social Class and I.Q. *Science*, 1971, *174*, 1285–1295.

Skodak, M. and Skeels, H., A Final Follow-Up Study of 100 Adopted Children. *Journal of Genetic Psychology*, 1949, *75*, 85.

Waddington, C. H., *The Strategy of the Genes*. London: Allen and Unwin, 1957.

7

CAN SLUM CHILDREN LEARN?

BY STEPHEN P. STRICKAND

Disadvantaged children may be capable of educational achievements far beyond anything heretofore imagined if a remarkable project in Milwaukee is the guide it clearly seems to be.

In the project, now in its fifth year, children from poor, illiterate parents living in the city's most depressed section have shown sustained high performance on a variety of tests administered from infancy through their fourth year. During that period, the youngsters' intelligence quotients jumped by better than 50 percent, with some of them achieving as high as 135.

This and other evidence gathered during the project seems to demonstrate that while early environmental circumstances have a powerful impact on a child's intellectual growth, the slum environment form a lifetime trap for the disadvantaged.

Taken alone, that finding may not seem novel, although convictions about the success of various educational "intervention strategies" sometimes have appeared to be based more on hope and sympathy than on scientific evidence. The Milwaukee Project provides hard data to support the belief that, under the right circumstances, intervention can be successful even in the most difficult situations. Beyond that, the Project suggests that some factors affecting learning capability and intelligence quotients, which at first glance could be interpreted as matters of inheritance, are rather matters of environment.

The implication of the latter finding is one of the things that makes the Milwaukee Project important. In fact, the Project's implications relate to several educational concerns from compensatory education to mental retardation. Broadly, they justify our paying greater attention to the availability, the kind, and the quality of education programs for the young child.

The Milwaukee Project was launched in 1964 when a multidisciplinary team from the University of Wisconsin under the direction of Rick Heber, Professor of Education and Child Psychology, began a series of surveys designed to learn more about the relationship of poverty to mental retardation. The team included professionals from the fields of psychology, psychiatry, sociology and speech therapy as well as education.

The Wisconsin group knew that by some estimates more than six million persons in the United States are considered to be mentally retarded and that, although the great majority of them have no identifiable. pathology of the nervous system, all have exceptionally low I.Q.'s and are functionally, if not physiologically, retarded. They also knew that mentally retarded persons are found in particularly large numbers among the populations of economically distressed urban rural areas. What had not been documented was a view that was nevertheless gaining increasing acceptance: that the retardation so frequently encountered in the slum was produced by the overall environment characteristically found there—a combination of ignorance, illiteracy, malnutrition, and economic, mental, and psychological depression.

That view overlooked two rather obvious facts: by far the great majority of disadvantaged persons living in slum areas are not retarded, and the majority of children reared by economically disadvantaged families develop and learn in a relatively normal fashion. These facts suggested that the heavy concentrations of mentally retarded persons in slum areas were related to certain specific factors rather than the general environment, and the Wisconsin group set out to find them.

The area selected for the surveys was that residential section of Milwaukee which, according to census data, had the lowest median family income, the greatest population density per housing unit, and the most dilapidated housing in the city. It was, in short, a classic urban slum. And predictably, it yielded a much higher rate of mental retardation among school children than any other area of the city.

The first survey was conducted in 1964, with all families in the area whose children included a newborn child being invited to participate. The most important finding to emerge from that initial study was that maternal intelligence was the most reliable single indicator of the level and character of intellectual development of the children. Although mothers with an I.Q. below 80 made up less than half the total group of mothers in the study, they accounted for about four-fifths of the children with I.Q.'s below 80. The survey data further showed that the lower the mothers' I.Q., the greater the possibility of their children scoring low on intelligence tests.

Fathers were not evaluated in the first survey. In a second survey, focused on 519 new-born infants in the area, intelligence tests were given to fathers, mothers, and children over two years of age. While the results showed that the father's intelligence level tended to be strikingly close to that of the mother, members of the team felt that the constant proximity of infant and mother and the fact that often the father did not reside in the home made maternal I.Q. a more dependable gauge.

As a result of their surveys and analyses, the University of Wisconsin group became convinced that the exceptional prevalence of mental retardation in the slums of American cities is not randomly distributed or randomly caused. Rather, it is concentrated within individual families that can be identified on the basis of maternal intelligence. In other words, the reason for the unusually high concentration of mental retardation in slum areas is not the slum environment generally, but the retarded parent residing in that environment.

Examined superficially, the population survey data from the Milwaukee study could be taken as suggestive evidence that "cultural-familial" mental retardation is more a matter of heredity than of environment. But what the team of educatorcholars actually observed in their repeated visits with hundreds of families was that the mentally retarded mother creates a social environment for her offspring that is distinctly different from that created by her neighbor of normal intelligence level.

Challenged by that observation, Heber and his associates determined to discover whether the kind of retardation that perpetuates itself from parent to child in the slum-dwelling family could be prevented, and if so, how. Under the auspices of the university and with grant support from the Social and Rehabilitation Service of the U.S. Department of Health, Education, and Welfare, the multidisciplinary team established an Infant Education Center in 1966 in the area where their surveys had been conducted. Knowing that only children of mothers with I.Q.'s less than 80 show a progressive decline in mean intelligence as they grow older, the Wisconsin group decided to focus their attention and their efforts on such youngsters. They wanted to work with children who, according to the record, were virtually certain to show characteristics of mental retardation as they grew older.

The challenge was to see whether intellectual deficiency might be prevented—as opposed to cured or remediated later—by introducing an array of positive factors in the children's early life, displacing factors that appeared to be negative or adverse. The Wisconsin team knew that any sound conclusions would have to be based on data developed over a period of years and for a relatively stable population group.

The teachers in the Milwaukee Project are both men and women and come from many different backgrounds. Not all of them are teachers by training. Indeed, not all of them have college degrees. They are chosen by the project directors from many applicants on the basis of personal interviews as well as comprehensive written information. What is sought is an ability for sensitive interaction with infants and small children and an ability to work within a system of special instruction that is both structured and flexible, requiring both discipline and initiative. Each teacher undergoes eight months of training before

153

beginning work at the Infant Education Center. (At present six of the nine teachers teaching the two-to-four-years-olds have been with the program from its early days.)

For the last four years some 40 mothers with I.Q.'s of less than 70 have, with their new-born children, participated in the Infant Education Center Project. When asked if they wished to have their children take part in such a program, all mothers who were offered the opportunity seized it quickly. The new-born babies of these mothers were divided into two groups, with two-thirds of them being placed in the experimental program and the remaining one-third in a control group. Beginning in the first few weeks of life, the project team launched a comprehensive "intervention" into the lives of those infants in the experimental program.

Shortly after the mother returned from the hospital, teachers began visiting the home for several hours each day, focusing most of their attention on the baby. Some weeks later, as soon as the mother and the teacher together decided that the time was right, mother and child joined programs at the Center. The infant child, usually three to four months old, was exposed to mental stimulation of a wide variety for several hours each day under a one-to-one ratio with trained adults. Meanwhile, the mother was encouraged, but not required, to take part in a center program designed to teach her improved home-making and baby-care techniques and, in some cases, to provide basic occupational training.

The oldest children are now moving toward their fifth birth-days. For the last four-and-a-half years they have been picked up early each morning at their homes and brought to the Center. Each child in the school has his own teacher until he is 2 months old. At that point, small group learning begins, with two-year-olds being placed in a class with five other youngsters. When the children are three years old, the size of the class is increased to eight; when they are four it's increased to 11. Throughout, three teachers are assigned to each class. This formula enables every teacher to specialize in a given area—reading, language development and expression, or mathematics—

154

while providing a constant relationship between each child and several adults and constant relationship among the children.

The education program is made up of a series of activities including important aspects of sensory and language stimulation. These activities are precisely structured, though the setting is arranged to encourage flexibility and initiative by both the infant and the teacher.

The schedule during four days of each week is firmly set for the children two years old and older. They arrive at the center by 9 a.m., and after they are given breakfast, they begin their classes at 9:30. Each of the three teachers engages a third of the pupils in learning activities in his or her special area, using both standard equipment and techniques, materials, and methods that have been developed at the center. For example, the Peabody Language Development Kit for primary level is used for children two, three, and four years old in their afternoon group language class. In the more individualized morning language class, the teacher usually uses equipment and methods developed over the last several years by Heber and his colleagues, and she may occasionally adapt variations from standard methods and equipment for particular purposes.

In his language class which lasts a half-hour, a child is guided by the teacher for 20 minutes of stimulatory exercises; in the remaining 10 minutes he may use the equipment or materials or continue, in any way he wishes, the activity the teacher began. His second class, also of a half-hour's duration, is likewise divided into 20 minutes of structured activity and 10 minutes of unstructured continuation of that activity. After a half-hour of free play, a third half-hour class brings the children to 11:30, when they decide whether they wish to watch "Sesame Street" on television—which the Milwaukee Project professionals rate highly—or continue one of the activities begun previously that morning.

155

After lunch and a nap, there are two additional classes in the afternoon, once more of a half-hour duration each. For these two classes, each age group is divided into two sessions with one teacher working with three to six children. The group language class emphasizes communication and problem-solving. The teacher might ask, for example, "What if you woke up in the morning and could find only one shoe?" The point is to stir the children's imaginations and encourage free verbalization of thought. A second teacher engages her section in lessons on topics that vary from week to week and include science, art, and music. As in the morning classes, there are 20 minutes of structured activity and 10 minutes of free use of equipment or free exploration of topics introduced earlier. Meanwhile, the third teacher uses this period to work individually with any child needing special help in any subject.

Both the morning and afternoon class groupings are based on a combination of ability and behavior. Hence there is, once more, flexibility within the structure. A child may have his language class at 9:30 on some days and at 11 on other days. For children less than two years old, the day's activities are not as structured as they are for the older youngsters. And on Friday's the day is less structured for all the children, often allowing for such special occasions as field trips.

The program for mothers continues after the children have begun their classes at the Center. Following the initial emphasis on child care and home-making, the program offers opportunities for vocational training and has assisted a number of mothers to secure steady employment for the first time. The Center does not employ any of the mothers but supports an active parents organization in which the majority of them participate.

From the very beginning of their participation in the infant education program the youngsters have been tested as well as taught. At given intervals a number of experimental measures of learning and performance—in language development and motor skills, among other areas—have been applied and standardized tests of intelligence and intellectual development administered.

156

Starting when they were 18 months old and continuing at six-week intervals thereafter, the children have been given a series of language performance tests, including both "free speech samples" (recordings of their conversations made at random intervals) and formal language tests. Over a period of three years, striking differences have developed in the performances of children in the experimental group and those in the control group. When the children in the experimental group reached 19 to 25 months of age, their vocabulary production did not begin in any instance until the child was 28 months old, and a number of the control group children still could not speak at that age.

An interesting phenomenon the University of Wisconsin team observed was that at approximately 28 months the children in the experimental group seemed to reach a vocabulary plateau lasting for one to two months. At that stage, as the children began to concentrate on grammatical structure, they produced fewer new words. Three or four months later, however, the children in the active program were able to express themselves in full sentences, some relatively complex, while most of the children in the control group were for the most part still producing unconnected words.

The children in the active stimulation program advanced rapidly not only in expression but in comprehension as well. A test given first at 36 months and thereafter at three-month intervals measured the children's comprehension of 16 different grammatical features or rules of the English language. At every point, the children in the experimental group showed significantly superior performance.

Indeed, on a whole range of tests—from simple matching and sorting to comprehension and motor skills to tests of intellectual development and intelligence quotient—the children who have been exposed since infancy to the daily routine of mental stimulation have shown remarkable development in contrast with the children in the control group. This holds true even when the performance of the experimental group is measured against the norms established by age peers generally.

Naturally, it was hoped and expected that the concentrated, carefully constructed program of stimulation of which one group of children was to be exposed would result in some noticeable differences. But the original specific goal was to test ways of preventing decline in intellectual development in children for whom such decline was predictable on a variety of grounds. What was not anticipated by Heber and his colleagues was the marked acceleration in a range of intellectual skills that has in fact occurred over the last four years on the part of the children in the experimental program.

Those differences are dramatized in the finding that at 42 months of age, the children in the active stimulation program measured an average of 33 I.Q. points higher than the children in the control group, with some of them registering I.Q.'s as high as 135. Equally remarkable, the children in the experimental program are learning at a rate that is in excess of the norm for their age peers generally.

The results of four years of effort and analysis that have gone into the Milwaukee Project obviously are extremely promising. The professional educators, social scientists, and teachers involved are nevertheless cautious in their interpretation of those results. For one thing, they want to collect and analyze data on the children participating in the project for another two years or more.

Further, the children have doubtless become "test wise," and the project team would like more time to assess the possible effect of this kind of sophistication. Nevertheless, the children in the control group have been tested as often as those in the experimental program, and so the difference in their performances obviously results from differences in their educational environment.

Whatever their caution, members of the University of Wisconsin group do say that, as far as they know, the intellectual stimulation and training given the children in the Milwaukee Project have been more comprehensive and intensive than that to which

158

any comparable groups of infants have ever been exposed. In the course of their efforts, members of the team have developed particular techniques—especially in the area of verbal skill development and reading comprehension—that seem to have affected the progress of the children, though team members are reluctant to suggest that those techniques and approaches are unique or even completely novel. They are, in any case, planning a series of instructional materials based on their research and teaching experience in infant education.

Despite the scientific caution and personal modesty of the Wisconsin group, their excitement at the possibilities they have developed shows through.

"We have seen a capacity for learning on the part of extremely young children that previously I would not have believed possible," says Heber. "While the results are by no means fully conclusive and must continue to be tested, the least that I am willing to say is that it is difficult to conceive of the children in the experimental program ever falling back to the level of their age peers in the lagging control group."

In any case, the trend of the data being developed in the Milwaukee Project engenders real hope that mental retardation of the kind that occurs in children whose parents are poor and of poor ability can be prevented. If the effort is begun early and remains constant in the early years, even very serious kinds of mental and intellectual disadvantage can possibly be forestalled.

SELECTED BIBLIOGRAPHY

Altman, J. & Das, G. D. Autoradiographic examination of the effects of enriched environment on the rate of glial multiplication in the adult rat brain. *Nature*, 1964, *204*.

Altus, W. D. Birth order and its sequelae. *Science*, 1966, *151*.

Altus, W. D. The American-Mexican: the survival of a culture. *J. Soc. Psychol.*, 1949.

Anastasi, A., *Differential Psychology* (3rd ed.) N.Y.: Macmillan, 1958.

Anastasi, A. Intelligence and family size. *Psychol. Bull.*, 1956, *53*.

Anastasi, A. & Drake, J. An empirical comparison of certain techniques for estimating the reliability of speed tests. *Educational and Psychological Measurement,* 1954, *14.*

Bajema, C. J. Estimation of the direction and intensity of natural selection in relation to human intelligence by means of the intrinsic rate of natural increase. *Eugen. Quart.,* 1963, *10.*

Bajema, C. J. Relation of fertility to educational attainment in a Kalamazoo public school population: a follow-up study. *Eugen. Quart.* 1966, *13.*

Baldwin, A. L. *Behavior and Development in Childhood.* N.Y.: Dryden Press, 1955.

Baldwin, A. L., Kalhorn, J. and Breese, F. H., Patterns of parent behavior. *Psychological Monographs,* 1945, *58,* N. 3.

Ball, W. W. Rouse. Calculating Prodigies. *The World of Mathematics.* John R. Newman (Ed.), Simon & Schuster, 1956, v. 1.

Banfield, E. *The Unheavenly City,* Boston: Little-Brown, 1970.

Bayley, N. Research in child development: a longitudinal perspective. *Merrill-Palmer Quart. Behav. Development,* 1965, *11.*

Bayley, N. Comparison of mental and motor test scores for ages 1–15 months by sex, birth order, race, geographical location, and education of parents. *Child Development,* 1965, *36.*

Bayley, N. Behavioral correlates of mental growth: birth to thirty-six years. *Amer. Psychol.,* 1968, *23.*

Bennett, E. L., Diamond, M. C., Krech, D. & Rosenweig, M. R. Chemical and anatomical plasticity of the brain. *Science,* 146, No. 3644 (1964).

Bereiter, C. & Engelmann, S. *Teaching disadvantaged children in the pre-school.* Englewood Cliffs, N.J.: Prentice-Hall, 1966.

Bertalaffny, L. von. *Modern theories of development.* N.Y.: Harper & Bros. (Torchbook Ed.) 1962.

Bilodeau, E. A. (Ed.), *Acquisition of Skill.* N.Y.: Academic Press, 1966.

Binet, A. & Simon, T. Sur la nécessité d'établir un diagnostic scientifique des états inférieurs de l'intélligence. *Année Psychologique.* 1905, *11.*

Birch, H. & Gussuow, J. *Disadvantaged Children, Health, Nutrition and School Failure.* N.Y.: Harcourt Brace, 1970.

160

Blalock, H. M. *Causal Inferences in Nonexperimental Research.* Chapel Hill: University of North Carolina Press, 1964.

Bloom, B. S. *Stability and Change in Human Characteristics.* N.Y.: John Wiley & Sons Inc., 1964.

Bloom, B. S. & Broder, L. J. *Problem-solving Processes of College students.* Chicago: Univ. Chicago Press, 1950.

Brattgard, S. O. The importance of adequate stimulation for the chemical composition of retinal ganglion cells during early postnatal development. *Acta Radiological* (Stockholm), 1952. Supplement 96.

Brinkman, E. H. Programmed instruction as a means of improving spatial visualization. *J. Applied Psychol.,* 1966, *50.*

Brison, D. W. (Ed.) *Accelerated learning and fostering creativity.* Toronto Canada: Ontario Institute for Studies in Education, 1968.

Brison, D. W. & Hill, J. (Eds.) *Psychology and early childhood education.* Ontario Institute for Studies in Education, 1968. N. 4.

Bronfenbrenner, U. The psychological costs of quality and equality in education. *Child Development* 1967, *38.*

Bruner, J. *The Process of Education.* Cambridge, Mass.: Harvard University Press, 1962.

Burks, B. S. The relative influence of nature and nurture upon mental development: a comparative study of parent-foster child resemblance and true parent-true child resemblance. *Yearbk. Nat. Soc. Stud. Educ.* 1928, *27,* (1).

Buros, O. I. (Ed.) *The Sixth Mental Measurements Yearbook.* Highland Park, N.J.: Gryphon Press, 1965.

Burt, C. Class difference in general intelligence: 111. *Brit. J. Stat. Psychol.,* 1959, *12.*

Burt, C. Intelligence and social mobility. *Brit. J. Stat. Psychol.,* 1961, *14.*

Burt, C. Is Intelligence distributed normally? *Brit. J. Stat. Psychol.,* 1963, *16.*

Burt, C. Mental capacity and its critics. *Bull. Brit. Psychol. Soc.,* 1968, *21.*

161

Burt, C. The distribution of intelligence. *Brit. J. Psychol.,* 1957, *48.*

Burt, C. The genetic determination of differences in intelligence: a study of monozygotic twins reared together and apart. *Brit. J. Psychol.,* 1966, *57.*

Burt, C. The evidence for the concept of intelligence. *Brit. J. Educ. Psychol.,* 1955, *25.*

Burt, C. The inheritance of mental ability. *Amer. Psychol.,* 1958, *13.*

Burt, C. & Howard, M. The multifactorial theory of inheritance and its application to intelligence. *Brit. J. Stat. Psychol.,* 1956, *9.*

Burt, C. & Howard, M. The relative influence of heredity and environment on assessments of intelligence. *Brit. J. Stat. Psychol.,* 1957, *10.*

Caspari, Ernst. Genetic endowment and environment in the determination of human behavior: biological viewpoint. *American Educational Research Journal,* 1968.

Cattell, R. B. *Personality: A Systematical Theoretical and Factual Study.* New York: McGraw-Hill, 1950.

Cattell, R. B. Theory of fluid and crystallized intelligence: a critical experiment. *J. Educ. Psychol.,* 1963, *54.*

Cattell, R. B. *The Fight for our National Intelligence.* London: King, 1937.

Cattell, R. B. The multiple abstract variance analysis equations and solutions: For nature-nurture research on continuous variables. *Psychol. Rev.,* 1960, *67.*

Cavalli-Sforza, L. L. & Bodmer, W. F. *The Genetics of Human Populations.* Freeman, San Francisco, 1971.

Chomsky, N. I.Q. Tests, *Ramparts,* July, 1972.

Chow, K. L., Riesen, A. H., & Newell, F. W. Degeneration of retinal ganglion cells in infant chimpanzees reared in darkness. *J. Compar. Neur.,* 1957, *107.*

Churchill, J. A., Neff, J. W. & Caldwell, D. F. Birth, weight and intelligence. *Obstetrics and Gynecology,* 1966, *28.*

Cohen, David K. Does I.Q. matter? *Commentary,* N. 53, N. 4, April, 1972.

162

Coleman, J. S., et al. *Equality of Educational Opportunity*, U.S. Dept. HEW, 1966.

Cooper, R. & Zubek, J. Effects of enriched and restricted early environments on the learning ability of bright and dull rats. *Canad. J. Psychol.*, 1958, *12*.

Cravioto, J. Malnutrition and behavioral development in the preschool child. Pre-school child malnutrition. *National Health Science Public*, 1966, No. 1282.

Cravioto, J., DeLicardie, E. R. & Birch, H. G. Nutrition, growth and neurointegrative development: an experimental and ecologic study. *Pediatrics*, 1966, *38*.

Cronbach, L. J. *Essentials of Psychological Testing*. (3rd ed.) N.Y.: Harper & Row, 1969.

Cronbach, L. J. & Warrington, W. J. Time limit tests: estimating their reliability and degree of speeding. *Psychometrika*, 1951, *16*.

Darcy, N. T. Bilingualism and the measurement of intelligence: review of a decade of research. *J. Genetic Psychol.* 1963, *103*.

Davis, K. Final note on a case of extreme isolation. *Amer. J. Sociol.*, 1947, *57*.

Davis, F. B. The measurement of mental capacity through evoked-potential recordings. (Educational Records Bureau, Greenwich, Conn. 1971).

Dennis, W. The performance of Hopi Indian children on the Goodenough Draw-a-Man Test. *J. Compar. Psychol.*, 1942, *34*.

Deutsch, M., Katz, I. & Jensen, A. R. (Eds.) *Social class, race, and psychological development*. N.Y.: Holt, Rinehart & Winston, 1968.

Dobzhansky, T. Genetic differences between people cannot be ignored. *Scientific Res.*, 1968, *3*.

Dobzhansky, T. *Mankind Evolving*. New Haven: Yale Univ. Press, 1962.

Dobzhansky, T. On genetics, sociology, and politics. *Perspect. Biol. Med.*, 1968, *11*.

Donald, H. P. Evidence from twins on variation in growth and production in cattle. *Proceedings of the Tenth International Congress of Genetics*, 1958, V. 1.

163

Dreger, R. M. & Miller, K. S. Comparative psychological studies of Negroes and whites in the United States. *Psychol. Bull.*, 1960, 57.

Dreger, R. M. & Miller, K. S. Comparative psychological studies of Negroes and whites in the United States: 1959–1965. *Psychol. Bull.*, 1968 (Monogr. Suppl. 70, N. 3, Part 2).

DuBois, P. H. et al. Factor analysis and related techniques in the study of learning. *Wash. Univ. Conf. Report*, St. Louis, Mo. Feb. 1959, Office of Naval Research, Contract N. Nonr. 816 (02), Technical Report N. 7.

Duncan, O. D. Is the intelligence of the general population declining? *Amer. Sociol. Rev.*, 1952, 17.

Duncan, O. D., Featherman, D. L. & Duncan, B. Socioeconomic background and occupational achievement: extensions of a basic model. *Final Report, Project* No. 5-0074 (E0-191), U.S. Dept. HEW, Office of Education, Bureau of Research, May 1968.

Dunn, L. M. *Expanded manual, Peabody Picture Vocabulary Test.* Minneapolis: American Guidance Service Inc., 1965.

Durham Education Improvement Program Research 1966–1967 (a).

Durham Education Improvement Program Research 1966–1967 (b).

Dustman, R. E. & Beck, E. C. The visually evoked potential in twins. *Electroenceph. Clin. Neurophysiol.*, 1965, 19.

Eckland, B. K. Genetics and sociology: a reconsideration. *Amer. Soc. Rev.*, 1967, 32.

Eells, K. et al. *Intelligence and Cultural Differences.* Chicago: Univ. Chicago Press, 1951.

Elkind, D. Quantity conceptions in junior and senior high school students. *Child Development*, 1961, 32.

Elkind, D. Piaget and Montessori. *Harvard Educational Review*, 1967 (Fall).

Elkind, D., Barocas, R. & Rosenthal, B. Combinatorial thinking in children from children from graded and ungraded classrooms. *Perceptual and Motor Skills*, 1968, 27.

Erlenmeyer-Kimling, L. & Jarvik, L. F. Genetics and intelligence: a review. *Science*, 1963, 142.

164

Eysenck, H. J. *The I.Q. Argument: Race, Intelligence, and Education.* N.Y., The Library Press, 1971.

Falconer, D. S. *An introduction to Quantitative Genetics.* N.Y., Ronald Press, 1960.

Fantz, R. L. The origin of form perception. *Scientific American,* 204:5, May, 1961.

Fehr, F. S. Critique of Hereditarian Accounts. *Harvard Educational Review,* 1969, 39.

Freeman, R. A. Schools and the elusive average children concept. *Wall Street Journal,* July 8, 1968.

Fuller, J. L. & Thompson, W. R. *Behavior Genetics.* N.Y., Wiley, 1960.

Gagne, R. M. (Ed.) *Learning and individual differences.* Columbus, Ohio: Merrill, 1967.

Gates, A. I. & Taylor, G. A. An Experimental study of the nature of improvement resulting from practice in mental function. *J. Educ. Psychol.,* 1925, 16.

Geber, M. The psycho-motor development of African Children in the first year, and the influence of maternal behavior. *J. Soc. Psychol.,* 1958, 47.

Geber, M. & Dean, R. F. A. The State of development of newborn African children, *Lance,* 1957.

Gesell, Arnold, *Wolf-Children and Human-Children.* N.Y.: Harper & Bros., 1940.

Ghiselli, E. E. The measurement of occupational aptitude. *Univ. Calif. Publ. in Psychol.,* Vol. 8, N. 2, 1955. Berkeley, California.

Goodenough, F. L. New Evidence on environmental influence on intelligence. *Nat. Soc. Stud. Educ.,* 1940, 39, Part I.

Goodenough, F. L. *The Measurement of Intelligence by Drawings.* Yonkers-on-Hudson, New York: World Book Co., 1926.

Goodnow, Jacqueline J. & Bethon, G. Piaget's tasks: The effect of schooling and intelligence. *Child Development,* 1966, 37.

Gordon, E. W. & Wilkerson, D. A. *Compensatory Education for the Disadvantaged.* New York: College Entrance Examination Board, 1966.

165

Gordon, I. J. (ed.) *Reaching the Child through Parent Education: The Florida Approach.* Gainesville: Institute for Development of Human Resources, College of Education, Univ. Fla., 1969.

Gordon, M. M. *Assimilation in American Life.* New York: Oxford Univ. Press, 1964.

Guilford, J. P. *Fundamental Statistics in Psychology and Education.* New York: McGraw Hill, 1965.

Guilford, J. P. *The Nature of Human Intelligence.* New York: McGraw Hill, 1967.

Gulliksen, H. *Theory of Mental Tests,* N.Y.: John Wiley & Sons, 1950.

Harlow, H. F. & Harlow, M. K. The mind of man. *Yearbook of Science and Technology,* N.Y.: McGraw-Hill, 1962.

Harlow, H. F. The development of learning in the Rhesus monkey. *Amer. Sci.,* 1959, 47.

Harrell, R. F., Woodyard, E. & Gates, A. I. *The Effect of mother's diets on the intelligence of offspring.* N.Y.: Bureau of Publications, Teachers College, 1955.

Hebb, D. O. *The Organization of Behavior.* N.Y.: John Wiley & Sons, Inc., 1949.

Heber, R. *Rehabilitation of Families at Risk for Mental Retardation.* (Regional Rehabilitation Center, Univ. Wisconsin, 1969.)

Herrnstein, R. "I.Q." *The Atlantic,* September, 1971.

Hess, R. D. & Bear, R. M. (eds.) *Early Education.* Chicago: Aldine, 1968.

Hess, R. D. & Shipman, V. C. Early experience and the socialization of cognitive modes in children. *Child Development,* 1965, 36.

Higgins, J. R., Reed, S. & Reed, E. Intelligence and family size. A paradox resolved. *Eugen. Quart.,* 1962, 9.

Honzik, M. P. Developmental studies of parent-child resemblances in intelligence. *Child Develop.,* 1957, 28.

Humphreys, L. G. The organization of human abilities. *Amer. Psychologist,* 1962b, 17.

Hunt, J. McV. *Intelligence and experience.* N.Y.: Ronald Press, 1961.

166

Hunt, J. McV. Intrinsic motivation and its role in psychological development. *Nebraska Symposium on Motivation* 13, ed. David Levine, Lincoln U., Nebraska Press, 1965.

Hunter, Kristin. Pray for Barbara's baby. *Philadelphia Magazine,* Aug. 1968.

Husén, T. Abilities of twins. *Scand. J. Psychol.,* 1960, 1.

Itard, Jean. *The Wild Boy of Aveyron.* N.Y., 1932.

Jenks, C. *Inequality.* Bobbs-Merrill, 1972.

Jensen, A. R. How much can we boost I.Q. and scholastic achievement? *Harvard Educational Review,* Vol. 39, No. 1, Winter-Spring, 1969.

Jensen, A. R. Do schools cheat minority children? *Educational Research,* Nov., 1971.

Jepsen, N. P. & Brednose, G. V. Investigation into the age of mentally deficient women at their first delivery. *Acta. Psychiat. Scand.,* 1956, (Monogr. Supplement, 108).

Johanson, I. & Rendel, J. Studies on the variation in dairy traits of intact and split pairs of cattle twins under farm conditions. *Acta. Agricul. Scand.,* 1971, 21.

Juel-Nielsen, N. & Morgensen, A. Uniovular twins brought up apart. *Acta. Genetica,* 1957, 7.

Kagan, J. & Moss, H. A. *Birth to Maturity.* N.Y.: Wiley, 1962.

Karnes, M. B. *A new role for teachers: involving the entire family in the education of preschool disadvantaged children.* Urbana: Univ. Illinois, College of Education, 1969.

Kates, Solis, L., Kates, W. W. & M. J., Cognitive Processes in deaf and hearing adolescents and adults. *Psychol. Monogr.,* 1962, 76, No. 551.

Katz, M. *The 19th Yearbook of the National Council on Measurements in Education,* Ames, Iowa, 1962a.

Klaus, R. A. & Gray, S. The early training project for disadvantaged children: a report after five years. *Monographs of the society for Research in Child Development,* 1968, 33, No. 4.

Klausmeier, H. J. & Harris, C. N. (eds.) *Analyses of Concept Learning.* N.Y.: Academic Press, 1966.

167

Klineberg, O. *Negro Intelligence and Selective Migration.* N.Y.: Columbia Univ. Press, 1935.

Laurence, E. M. An investigation into the relation between intelligence and inheritance. *Brit. J. Psychol.* Monogr. Suppl., 1931, 16, No. 5.

Leahy, A. M. Nature-nurture and intelligence. *Genet. Psychol. Monogr.,* 1935, 17.

Lee, E. S. Negro Intelligence and selective migration: a Philadelphia test of the Klineberg hypothesis. *Amer. Sociol. Rev.,* 1951, 16.

Lee, U. The Employment of Negro Troops. U.S. Gov't. Printing Office, U.S. Army, Special Studies, 1966.

Lenski, G. *The Religious Factor.* N.Y.: Doubleday & Co., 1961.

Lerner, I. M. *Heredity, Evolution and Society.* San Francisco: W. H. Freeman & Co., 1968.

Lewontin, R. C. Race and Intelligence. *Bull. of Atomic Sci.,* March, 1970, 2–8. (Reprinted here)

Lesser, G. S., Fifer, G. & Clark, D. H. Mental abilities of children from different social-class and cultural groups. *Monogr. Soc. Res. Child Develop.,* 1965, 30, (4).

Loevinger, J. On the proportional contributions of differences in nature and nurture to differences in intelligence. *Psychol. Bull.,* 1943, 40.

Lord, F. M. A paradox in the interpretation of group comparisons. *Psychol. Bull,* V. 68, N. 5, 1969.

Mayeske, G. W. On the explanation of racial-ethnic group differences in achievement test scores. Paper presented for American Psychological Association Meeting, Wash., D.C., Sept., 1971.

Meade, J. E. & Parker, A. S. *Biological Aspects of Social Problems.* Edinburgh: Oliver & Boyd, 1966.

Mercer, J. R. Sociological perspectives on mild mental retardation: *in* H. Carl Haywood (ed.) *Social-cultural Aspects of Mental Retardation: Proceeding of the Peabody NIMH Conference.* New York: Appleton-Century-Crafts, Inc., 1970.

Mercer, J. R. Sociocultural factors in labeling mental retardates. *The Peabody Journal of Education.* April, 1971, 48 (3).

168

Mercer, J. R. Institutionalized Anglocentrism: Labeling mental retardates in the public schools: *in* Peter Orleans and William R. Eliss, Jr., (ed.), *Race, Change, and Urban Society: Urban Affairs Annual Review*, Vol. 5. Los Angeles: Sage Publications, Inc., 1971.

Mercer, J. R. Who is normal? Two perspectives on mild mental retardation. *Patients, Physicians and Illness* (Rev. ed.) E. G. Jaco (ed.). N.Y.: The Free Press of Glencoe, 1972.

Mercer, J. R. *Labeling the mentally retarded.* Berkeley: University of Calif. Press, 1972, in press.

Mitra, S. Income, socioeconomic status, and fertility in the United States. *Eugen. Quart.,* 1966, 13.

Minor, J. B. *Intelligence in the United States.* N.Y. Springer, 1957.

Montessori, M. *The Montessori Method.* N.Y.: Schocken, 1964.

Mowry, R. & Singh, J. A. L. *Wolf-Children and Feral Man.* Harper & Bros, N.Y. 1942.

Moynihan, D. P. *The Negro Family.* Office of Policy Planning and Research, U.S. Dept. of Labor, Wash. D.C., 1965.

National Academy of Sciences. Racial studies: Academy states position on call for new research. *Science,* 1967, 158.

Newman, H. H., Freeman, F. N. & Holzinger, K. J. *Twins: A Study of Heredity and Environment.* Chicago: Chicago Univ. Press, 1937.

Pettigrew, T. *A Profile of the Negro American.* Princeton, N.J.: Van Nostrand, 1964.

Piaget, J. *The Origins of Intelligence in Children.* N.Y.: International Universities Press, 1952.

Piaget, J. *Six Psychological Studies.* N.Y.: Random House, 1967.

Plotkin, L. Negro intelligence and the Jensen Hypothesis. *The N.Y. Statistician,* 1971, 22.

Racial and ethnic survey of California public schools, Part 1: Distribution of pupils, Fall, 1966, 1967, 1968, Sacramento: State Department of Education, 1966, 1967, 1968.

Raven, J. C. *Guide to the Standard Progressive Matrices.* London: H. K. Lewis & Co., Ltd., 1960.

Reed, E. W. & Reed, S. C. *Mental Retardation: A Family Study.* Phila.: W. B. Saunders Co., 1965.

Reiss, A. *Occupations and Social Status.* N.Y.: The Free Press, 1961.

Reymert, M. L. & Hinton, R. T., Jr., The effect of a change to a relatively superior environment upon the I.Q. of one hundred children. *Yearbk. Nat. Soc. Stud. Educ.,* 1940, 39 (1).

Roe, Arne. *The Making of a Scientist.* N.Y.: Dodd, Mead & Co., 1953.

Sarason, S., Davidson, K., Lighthall, F., Waite, R., Ruebush, B. *Anxiety in Elementary School Children.* N.Y.: John Wiley & Son, 1960.

Scarr-Salapatek, S. Unknowns in the I.Q. Equation. *Science,* 1971, 174.

Scarr-Salapatek, S. Race, Social Class and I.Q. *Science,* 1971, 174.

Schull, W. J. & Neel, J. V. *The Effects of Inbreeding on Japanese Children.* N.Y.: Harper & Row, 1965.

Schweel, M. *Who can be educated?* N.Y.: Grove, 1968.

Scrimshaw, N. S. Infant malnutrition and adult learning. *Saturday Review,* March 16, 1968.

Senna, C. *The Atlantic.* "Backtalk", December 1971, February 1972.

Shields, J. *Monozygotic Twins.* London: Oxford Univ. Press, 1962.

Shuey, A. M. *The testing of Negro Intelligence* (2nd ed.) N.Y.: Social Science Press, 1966.

Skeels, H. M. Adult status of children with contrasting early life experiences: A follow-up study. *Child Development Monogr.,* 1966, 31. (No. 3.)

Skeels, H. M. & Dye, H. B. A study of the effects of differential stimulation on mentally retarded children. *Proc. Addr. Amer. Assn. Ment. Defic.,* 1939, 44.

Skodak, M. & Skeels, H. M. A follow-up study of 100 adopted children. *J. Genetic Psychol.,* 1949.

Spuhler, J. N. & Lindzey, G. *Racial Differences in Behavior.* J. Hirsch (ed.), Behavior Genetic Analysis. N.Y.: McGraw-Hill, 1967.

Srole, L. Social integration and certain corrollaries: an explanatory study. *Amer. Soc. Review,* 1956, V. 21.

170

Stock, M. B. & Smyth, P. M. Does undernutrition during infancy inhibit brain growth and subsequent intellectual development? *Arch. Dos. Childh.*, 1963, 38.

Stoddard, G. D. *The Meaning of Intelligence.* N.Y.: Macmillan, 1943.

Stott, D. H., Interaction of heredity and environment in regard to measured intelligence. *Brit. J. Educ. Psychol.*, 1960, 30.

Strodtbeck, F. L. Family interaction, values and achievement in A. L. Baldwin, Urie Bronfenbrenner, D. C. McClelland, J. L. Strodtbeck: *Talent and Society.* Princeton, N.J.: Van Nostrand, 1958.

Terman, L. M. & Merill, M. A. *Stanford-Binet Intelligence Scale.* Boston: Houghton-Mifflin, 1960.

Thompson, W. R. The inheritance and development of intelligence. *Res. Publ. Assn. Nerv. Ment. Dis.*, 1954.

Thorndike, E. L. Measurement of Twins. *J. Philos. Psychol. Sc. Meth.*, 1905.

Turner, R. *The Social Context of Ambition.* San Francisco: Chandler Publishing Co., 1964.

U.S. Censuses of population and housing: 1960 Final report PHI (1)-135, census tract, San Bernadino-Riverside-Ontario, California Standard metropolitan statistical area. Washington, D.C.: U.S. Gov't Printing Office, 1962.

U.S. *Commission on Civil Rights, Racial Isolation in the public schools.* V. 1, Washington, D.C.: U.S. Gov't Printing Office, 1967.

U.S. Dept. H.E.W. Public Health Service, vital and health statistics, series 11-number 110. "Intellectual development of children by demographic and socioeconomic factors in the United States." Washington, D.C.: U.S. Gov't Printing Office, Dec., 1971.

Vernon, P. E. *Intelligence and Cultural Environment.* London: Methuen, 1969.

Vernon, P. E. Symposium on the effects of coaching and practice in intelligence tests. *Brit. J. Educ. Psychol.*, 1954, 24.

Waddington, C. H. *The Strategy of the Genes.* London: Allen & Unwin, 1957.

Walters, C. E. Comparative Development of Negro and white infants. *J. Genet. Psychol.*, 1967, 110.

Wechsler, D. *WISC manual, Wechsler intelligence scale for children*. N.Y.: The Psychological Corporation, 1949.

Wechsler, D. *The Measurement and Appraisal of Adult Intelligence* (4th ed.) Baltimore: Williams & Wilkins, 1958.

Williams, F. (ed.) *Language and Poverty*. Chicago: Markham, 1970.

Young, M. *The Rise of the Meritocracy*. London: Thames & Hudson, 1958.

NOTES ON CONTRIBUTORS

Christopher Jencks is a Professor of Education at Harvard University's Graduate School of Education. He co-authored THE ACADEMIC REVOLUTION with David Riesman and is the author of a recent book, *Inequality*.

David Layzer is Professor of Astronomy, Harvard College and has had long experience in the training of American astronomers and physicists.

Richard Lewontin is a Professor of Biology at the University of Chicago.

Professors Jane Mercer and Wayne Curtis Brown teach in the Sociology Department, University of California, Riverside.

David Robinson is Vice-President of the Carnegie Foundation.

Carl Senna was formerly director of a career and college counseling program serving the five predominantly black high schools in Boston. Presently he is a lecturer at the University of Massachusetts in Boston in the English and Humanities Departments.

Stephen Strickland is a former director of the National Advisory Council on the Education of Disadvantaged Children. He is presently a consultant in education and health and lives in Washington, D.C.

INDEX

Heber, R., 27, 45, 153, 158
heritable traits, ix, 9
hereditarian, xiii, 26, 43
hereditary (caste) aristocrats, 19,
    28
heredity
    and I.Q., 42 *see* I.Q.
    and intelligence, 1, *see*
      intelligence
heritability
    concept, 9, 89, 124, 134
    conventional application,
      15, 17, 123
    estimates, 10, 11, 100, 134,
      139, 147
    one estimate (Burt) of
      identical twins, 11
    irrelevance to I.Q. between
      populations, 13, 119
    meaning within a popula-
      tion, 13
    Studies, 84 *see* Studies,
      I.Q.
    approach of Jensen, x, 84,
      89 see Jensenism
Herrnstein, R., ix, 29, 48, 50, 52,
    84, 118, 128, 131, 137, 142,
    147
high I.Q. Blacks, 40 *see* I.Q.
high normals (I.Q.), 63 *see* I.Q.
home ownership (relation to I.Q.),
    78 *see* I.Q.
human intelligence (definitions), 50
    see intelligence
Hypothesis of fixed mental capacity,
    142, 144 *see* unlimited
    educability

I

identical twins, 85 *see* twins, Studies
idiot savants, 50
indicators of child's exposure to
    Anglo culture, 76
Individualistic Achievement Values,
    79
Indian caste, 30
Indo-European, 28
induction (reasoning), 52
Infant Educational Center, 153–158

inferences, (and scientific data), 52
information,
    genesis, 133
    processing ability, 132
    subtest, 67 *see* subtest
inheritance (genetic), 19, 36
Innocent, X., 1
intellectual capacity, 43, 45, 59
    potential, 33
    differences of potential, 58
intelligence
    atoms, 43
    arguments, 43, 100, 109
    Binet's label, 109
    biological potential, xi, 59
    (of) California Public
      School Children, 56
    cognitive development,
      132
    controversy, 48
    correlation to I.Q. test
      scores, 4, 45
    crystallized, 5
    data, 48
    fluid, 5
    general, 5
    genotype, 9, 10
    and heredity, 1
    human, 50 *see* human
      intelligence
    and I.Q., 24, 43
    and I.Q. differences, 43
    innate, 109
    nature of, 1, 4, 85–103
    Negro-white difference, 12
    objective measure of, 58
    quotient, 110
    quotient jump, 150
    and race, 1
    table, 74 *see* Tables
    tests, 146 *see* Tests
    test performance, 43
    (I.Q.) testing vs. Achieve-
      ment tests, 103
    intensive educational
      stimulation, 45,
      153–157
    interaction of genetics and
      environment, 134
I.Q.
    abnormal (high), (low),
      63

178

179

I.Q. (*continued*)
    within-ethnic-group differences (chart 2), 82
Itard, Jean, 53

J

Jansen, Cornelius, (Bishop of Ypres), 1
Jansenism, 1
Jencks, C., 24, 31–41
Jensen, A. R., ix–xv, 1, 2, 5–17
Jensenism, ix
Jewish children, 39
Jews vs Christian I.Q. scores, 41

L

Layzer, D., 114–147
Learning as a process of abstraction, 45
Lerner, I. M., 114, 120, 126
Lewontin, R. C., 1–17
logical system, 128
long headed people, 28
low I.Q. people, 29 *see* I.Q.
lower class, xii
Lysenko, T. D., x

M

manual dexterity, 67 *see* subtests
marriage controls, xi *see* eugenic planning
Marx, K., 1
mating, (role of I.Q.), 34 *see* I.Q.
maze puzzle, game (I.Q.), 47, 50 *see* I.Q.
mean (I.Q. scores), 110
    for Blacks and whites, 12 *see* I.Q.
    for three ethnic groups, 74
meaning of intelligence, 50 *see* intelligence
measures,
    conventional, 51 *see* conventional measures
    environmental variables, 36, 74, 81–82
mechanical ability, 67 *see* ability

mental ability, 5, 58 *see* ability
mental retardation, 47
    adaptive behavior, 47
    clinical definition, 57
    cultural familial, 152
    false labeling, 57
    I.Q. test scores (as symptoms), 57
    social symptoms, 47
mental testing movement, 32
Mercer, Jane R., 56–110
meritocracy, 52
Mexican-American, 53–54, note, 56
    Blacks and Anglos I.Q. correlations, 77 *see* correlations
Milwaukee Project
    see Studies
minority neighborhood, 56, 77
monozygotic (twins), 84 *see* one-egg twins (correlations)
Moynihan, D. P., xi *see* Negro Family Report
Moynihan's Report, xi
multiple correlations, 105
mutant genes, 8
myth of Black genetic mental inferiority, xiv
mystical Aryan blood, 28

Mc

McCarthy, Joseph, x *see* anti-Communist sentiment
McCarthyism, x
McLuhan, Marshall, 50

N

National Academy of Sciences, 1
National Center for Health Statistics, 98
native intelligence, 109 *see* intelligence
nature of intelligence, 50, 85–103 *see* intelligence
Negro, xii, 56 *see* Blacks, Afro-Americans
    and American Indians (I.Q. comparisons), 13, 14, 39, 48